Praise for **Big Freakin' Change**

AF091485

"*Big Freakin' Change* is must-read for anyone who wants to make change and feel more confident. This game-changing book reveals the truth about what keeps us feeling stuck and waiting to feel ready. It is a transformative guide that will help you flex your courage muscle and learn how to take action one step at a time."

ERIN SKYE KELLY, award-winning and
bestselling author of *Naked Money Meetings*

"I love what Cara Moeller Poppitt is doing for women and girls by letting them know they are ready for success! She explains that so often we feel paralyzed by doubt and the need for perfection that we never take that first step to reach our dreams. *Big Freakin' Change* is a practical how-to guide that recognizes that confidence is gained through the actions we take toward our goals, even if we stumble and fail on the way. We just have to start!"

HON. RONA AMBROSE, founder
and chair of the Council of Women CEOs

"Whether you're interested in making a change in your work, your relationships, your environment, your mindset, your purpose in life and how you fulfill that purpose—or any other big change—Cara Moeller Poppitt has a proven method to help you on your path forward, to step out and step into the next version of yourself."

MARGARET ANDREWS, Harvard instructor
and founder of The MYLO Center

"*Big Freakin' Change* is a true reset for how we define courage and access it within ourselves. This book will expand your capacity by reconnecting you at a deeper level with the confidence and courage that is always within."

PENNY ZENKER, keynote speaker and
USA Today-bestselling author of *The Reset Mindset*

"*Big Freakin' Change* is a powerful guide for any woman ready to take bold steps toward the life she dreams of. Whether you're pursuing a passion, redefining your purpose, or finding joy in the journey, this book will remind you that you are capable of massive, meaningful change. It's not just a book—it's a catalyst for your next big move."
CONNIE JAKAB, mental health and belonging specialist

"If you are feeling stuck yet know deep down that there is something bigger out there for you, *Big Freakin' Change* is the book for you! Cara Moeller Poppitt has worked with girls and women for decades helping them to see and create new possibilities in their lives. Her passion and enthusiasm leap off the page as she shares stories of personal transformation, career pivots, and letting go of limiting beliefs."
ELLEN CONNELLY TAAFFE, Kellogg School of Management professor and award-winning author of *The Mirrored Door*

"*Big Freakin' Change* is a breath of fresh air. Cara Moeller Poppitt has eloquently captured the root of what stops women from stepping into change and more importantly provides a simple and clear framework for upgrading and transforming our lives from the inside out. If you feel like you were made for more than just existing, get into this book and follow her process. Magic awaits you."
KELSEY GRANT, songwriter, love coach, and cofounder of *Club Unhinged*

**BIG
FREAKIN'
CHANGE**

CARA MOELLER POPPITT

BIG

FREAKIN'

How to Gain Confidence by Stepping Out Before You Are Ready

CHANGE

Copyright © 2025 by Cara Moeller Poppitt

All rights reserved. No part of this book may be reproduced, stored in a retrieval system or transmitted, in any form or by any means, without the prior written consent of the publisher or a license from The Canadian Copyright Licensing Agency (Access Copyright). For a copyright license, visit accesscopyright.ca or call toll free to 1-800-893-5777.

Some names and identifying details have been changed to protect the privacy of individuals.

The Get Unstuck, Cycle of Change Model™ is a registered trademark of Cara Moeller Poppitt.

Cataloguing in publication information is available from Library and Archives Canada.
ISBN 978-1-77458-558-0 (paperback)
ISBN 978-1-77458-565-8 (ebook)

Page Two
pagetwo.com

PAGE TWO™ is a trademark owned by Page Two Strategies Inc., and is used under license by authorized licensees

Cover and interior design by Fiona Lee
Interior illustrations by Michelle Clement and Fiona Lee

Distributed in Canada by Raincoast Books
Distributed in the US and internationally by Macmillan

25 26 27 28 29   5 4 3 2 1

bigfreakinchange.com

Dedicated to my children: Caden, Jordan & Claire.

*May you always have courage
to follow your dreams and embrace change.*

CONTENTS

Author's Note *1*

1 **The Change You Want** *5*

2 **Courage to Change** *29*

3 **Types of Change** *45*

4 **Update Your Mindset** *67*

5 **Small Steps, Massive Change** *93*

6 **Rest, Reflect, Protect** *117*

7 **Act Boldly** *141*

8 **Joy in the Journey** *161*

9 **Unlock Your Confidence** *177*

10 **Stepping Into Greatness** *199*

Acknowledgments *223*

Notes *225*

Hey, beautiful,

I am so glad you are here.

Over the last fifteen years, I've worked with over forty thousand girls and women in my dance studio and through business coaching. I've watched so many of them make big changes in their lives and be changed in the process. Through this experience, I've come to believe that there's no more powerful force, or greater potential for good, than a woman who gives herself permission to hold on to a big dream. And then achieves it.

I see it on the dance floor every day, as young girls take step after step into their dream of learning to dance. For some girls, learning the basics is the dream itself. For others, that's only the beginning; learning to dance transforms into a passion from which other dreams are born. I love watching that process and seeing the girls develop so many skills along the way that will serve them in pursuing their dreams in the future: confidence, determination, and courage.

Step by step by step.

I also see it in my coaching clients as I work with entrepreneurs to reach new levels of success. These fierce and brilliant women take step after step into *their* dreams. Businesses are started, careers are changed, new passions are fanned into flame, and new relationships are formed.

Step by step by step.

This is a book about making big changes in your life in pursuit of a dream or a desire, *even when you don't feel ready* and *especially when you feel stuck*. Nobody picks up a book like this unless they have already the *desire* and therefore the *potential* to take the next step. Although we all have the capacity for big dreams, so often they disintegrate into more "realistic" versions with the passing of time and the challenges of life. Sometimes it feels like we've lost our ability to dream altogether. Without a dream, and the hope that it gives us for a more brilliant future, we feel lost, stuck, disconnected, and unfulfilled. Getting unstuck starts with a step forward. I've seen how young girls develop their skills and transform into confident and powerful young women, and how women turn into powerful wise women by owning their brilliance.

And then there is you. I wrote this book with you in mind. Although we probably haven't met yet, I imagined you when I sat down every day to write. My hope is that the message in this book will play a small role in helping you reach your fullest potential.

Perhaps you're feeling stuck in one area of your life. Heck, maybe you're feeling stuck in *every* area of your life. I want you to know that's okay. I have been there more times than I count, and so has pretty much every woman, ever. It's normal. We just don't talk about it.

I remember what it felt like to look at my life at the ripe age of seventeen and think, "Is this all there is?" even after making an adventurous move to Mexico by myself. Or worse: "Is this all it will *ever* be?" when I landed my dream job but still dreamed about becoming an entrepreneur with my own business.

I know what it feels like to be stuck in place, waiting indefinitely for that elusive feeling of "being ready" to kick in and carry me to my next destination. I remember well how it felt before I opened my businesses, waiting to feel ready.

I know what it feels like to be totally caught up in the busyness of life raising three children in my thirties, so much so that I couldn't even *remember* what my dream used to be or, worse yet, who I even was.

I also know what it's like to have a dream so big that the magnitude of it makes you freeze up, with no idea how to move even an inch in the right direction. I know what it feels like to doubt yourself and think you are an imposter when you try to step up. I have had this feeling as I wrote this book and as I struggle to learn the skills I need to serve others now that I'm in my forties.

And I know what it's like to be moving toward a big dream, stepping out on large stages to speak only to get the wind kicked out of me, and to wonder if I'll ever be able to dream again. This is the version of myself that I am currently navigating. Our challenges may vary, but I am certain our insecurities are the same. We are more similar than we are different.

My life is not perfect, and I have lots of messy parts like everyone else, but I move through change differently now and I have helped many girls and women do so too. Let's face it: standing out on a stage to dance or on the stage of life takes courage, clarity, and confidence. I have found a way to help girls and women find these qualities and take center stage in their own lives without waiting to feel ready. This is *a guide for making change*, and I'm talking about big freakin' changes.

You'll learn how to choose the changes you want in your life and step into them with confidence—*even when you have no confidence at all.*

This book is not intended to be a collection of ideas that only inspire you. It's meant to be a catalyst you can use to change the course of your life forever. Any kind of change is possible if you tap into the courage that is already inside you.

It won't give you a quick fix but a path to becoming a work in progress, giving you momentum to take action and make the change you want in your life, so you can live an even more remarkable one. You should also know that it will only work for you *if you take action*. There is no alternative, and no one can do the work for you. It always starts with starting.

If you read this book and take action as you go, I will teach you the skills to connect to your mind, body, and soul in a new way to get better results. I hope it will be the last book you'll need to read to get unstuck and move forward. My dream is that it will give you back your wings to fly, and you will take greater chances on yourself and reach new heights. I hope you give yourself permission to change and develop the skill set to change. I also hope you bust a big freakin' move on a dance floor and feel awesome doing it.

Here's the thing: change is inevitable. We are supposed to change, but this was a foreign concept to the generations who came before us. Women especially were not encouraged to change, and so the uneasy feelings about change are real and hard for all of us. But think about it: change is found everywhere in nature. Our bodies have cycles, the seasons have cycles, the stars have cycles, and the nature of change is cyclical as well. We can't escape change, but we can master the art of it, and we can choose how we navigate change so that it lifts us up and adds value to the people around us.

Once you understand the Get Unstuck, Cycle of Change Model™ that I share in this book, it becomes clear that we can all set the stage for massive, positive change in our lives. If we don't understand it, it's really easy to feel stuck and stay stuck. We will find reasons and excuses to justify why we are stuck in life. Stuck in a job that we hate. Stuck in a relationship that doesn't serve us. Stuck in a mindset that brings us down. Stuck in a belief that keeps us frozen in time. And stuck in a story that limits us. When we feel stuck, it's easy to lose hope and become a passive witness to our life, watching and wishing and waiting for it to be different.

Whether you want to change your career, your finances, your location, your relationships, or your identity, the first thing you need to change is your relationship with change itself.

I don't know your past or what you have been through, but I know the hearts of thousands of women just like you, and I know you are here for a reason. You are on the verge of stepping into the next version of yourself. You want to make a change and not a small one—a big one. I call that a Big Freakin' Change. Welcome to the next version of yourself. It's only a few steps away.

You've got this!

Cara

P.S. after each chapter, you can visit bigfreakinchange.com for a deeper dive.

1
THE CHANGE YOU WANT

"You gain strength, courage, and confidence by every experience in which you really stop to look fear in the face... You must do the thing you think you cannot do."

ELEANOR ROOSEVELT

As I prepared a few of my dancers for their solo competition, they all had the familiar telltale signs of fear: wide eyes, set jaws, and fidgeting hands.

"Focus on your craft and your performance," I told them. "That's *it*."

Tamia was in the wings, about to go onstage. She is a natural powerhouse of a dancer who executes on every level. She is technically very strong and beautiful to watch. Still, her eyes were glued to her competitors. She seemed smaller somehow, closed in on herself. I'd seen this situation unfold countless times with dancers of every level of experience.

Tamia was stuck.

Sometimes a dancer freezes, and they can't go onstage at all. If they do manage to push themselves onstage, they hold back and just go through the motions. They don't bring it—their power, their joy, or their essence. They lack confidence, and it shows in their performance.

I gently touched Tamia's shoulder. "Let yourself go. Be more relaxed, wilder, and enjoy yourself."

Usually, it's the other way around and I have to remind my students to remember their technique. Tamia needed to give herself permission to let go of her body and anything negative in her head holding her back, like comparing herself to others or feeling not good enough.

"You've done all the work," I said. "You've got this, girl. You're prepared. Now it's time to enjoy." Then I added, "You are ready."

With those three words, Tamia's shoulders dropped instantly, her breathing slowed down, and her nervous smile turned into a determined grin. She stood taller. Her eyes changed, and her energy expanded.

When she stepped onstage to do her Tina Turner dance in her black sequined outfit, she was on fire. That day, she won top soloist in a competition of more than one thousand entrants.

As a dance studio owner, choreographer, and teacher, I've worked with over thirty thousand dancers to get them to take center stage and step out of the wings. As a business coach, I have witnessed thousands of women be held back by fear and wait to feel ready before they make a move or take a chance. They all wait for a sign that gives them permission to step out and be brave. All of them wait to feel ready. My guess is you too are waiting to feel ready.

You've been wanting to make a change for a while now. You want more or new or better. More joy, more love, more meaning. A new relationship, a new baby, or a new career. A better education, better health, or a better bottom line. You have a dream for your future, and you know you need to take the first step, but something has been holding you back.

You don't feel ready yet.

And so you wait.

You wait until you get all your ducks in a row.

Until you have the right qualifications and enough experience.

Until you've lost the weight and gained the approval.

Until you have more time, more energy, more money.

You wait until you've researched all your options, weighed the pros and cons, lined up all your resources.

Until you're sure your loved ones can handle the change.

Until you're sure you will not fail. Or until you give yourself permission to go.

If any of this sounds familiar, you are in good company. I get it. When I was a professional dancer, appearing in music videos, showcases, and television commercials, I spent a lot of time waiting in the wings. I waited backstage just behind the curtains for my music cue to come onstage and dance. When I heard my cue, I moved.

On the stage of life, many of us wait in the wings for the cue that tells us we are finally ready to step out—to start a business, start a family, start working on an "impossible" dream. But that cue is not a note in a song; it's not easy to hear. Even if we think we hear it, we don't trust it. Because often we don't trust *ourselves*. We are scared to change, to let go of the old in order to welcome the new.

So we wait to be ready, to feel confident enough to move forward. We wait. And wait. And wait.

The sad reality is that many people wait in the wings of life forever and never step out. They are stuck waiting forever. Or they just give up, believing their goal is out of reach.

I have witnessed thousands of girls and women waiting in the wings—to dance onstage or to make a change in life. Every single one of them wants to feel ready before they begin. It starts as children and stays with us into adulthood without us noticing. It happens automatically to all of us until we deliberately choose to step out and create something better for ourselves.

I see it every day. So many women feel lost, stuck, disconnected, or unfulfilled. They wonder what is wrong with them. They are hard on themselves. They never feel quite good enough. They worry about judgment from others and wonder if they'll ever have what it takes to step out. All the waiting to be ready has eroded their confidence. They feel so much fear: fear of the unknown, fear of failure, and even the fear of success.

Feeling stuck is normal, and if you feel that way, *you* are normal.

You didn't do anything wrong and more importantly nothing is wrong with you.

And you haven't missed your window for change.

You still have time to take your cue and step out from the wings onto the stage of life.

This book will help you do just that. One step at a time.

Why Women Wait

All people, regardless of gender, are hardwired for safety, not success. Our brains prefer to keep everything in our life consistent and avoid loss. It's not just that we are scared of change, but psychology shows we are scared of loss. Taking a risk, stepping out onto the stage—that is scary, so no wonder you don't feel ready. Neuroscience suggests that the human brain is a prediction machine in search of the familiar. Waiting in the wings (our comfort zone) is familiar, and stepping out to make change is vulnerable, unpredictable, and uncertain.

Women are more likely to wait to move forward than men. We tend to put ourselves as our *last* priority on a long list of things to do; we never squeeze in the time for us. We are biologically wired and taught to be nurturers. We feel guilty for taking time for ourselves, and we put our goals on the back burner, waiting to feel ready and for the perfect time. We wait for things to change and hope that things will get better. We people-please, and we're uncomfortable with setting healthy boundaries or taking time to take care of ourselves. Most of us haven't seen many women role-modeling this. Our roles have evolved, and we are all doing our very best to manage the many responsibilities we hold. We are on the verge of making change, if only we knew how. And while the world around us chips away at our confidence, we simultaneously wait to feel ready and good enough before taking action. And so, many of us end up waiting forever, watching others from the sidelines of life. We fail to step into our brilliance, ignoring our goals and failing to reach our potential. It's not just you or me; it's all of us. The stats are stacked up against us, and the gap is not closing anytime soon.

You've heard the stats. Women are paid less than men, only making 83 percent of what men make. Women apply for jobs only when they meet at least 85 percent of the criteria, whereas men apply when meeting only 50 percent. Women are less likely to start businesses, but make up 40 percent of entrepreneurs. Research suggests that less than 9 percent of small businesses break one million dollars in revenue, and *Forbes* states that less than 2 percent of all businesses are women-owned. I am proud and grateful to belong to this group of women, and it's all because I learned how to embrace change.

Another article in *Forbes* notes, according to the UN Women's most recent report, "at the current rate of progress, it will take 286 years for the world to achieve gender equality. Per the World Economic Forum it will take another 132 years to close the global gender gap." The list goes on, and the stats continue to come out, highlighting the differences between women and men.

But do we even need those statistics? Really?

As women, we know exactly what it's like. We live in a culture that seems to always expect more of us, and yet we're supposed to expect less in return. We have to hustle more, or we're lazy. But we have to prioritize self-care, or we're not taking care of ourselves. We have to put up with more, or we're complaining. We have to speak up more, or we're overlooked. We have to be nurturing, or we're not kind enough. But we can't be too nurturing, or we're overbearing. We have to look great, or we're not good enough. But we can't look *too* great, or we're high maintenance. We can feel like we are too much in one area or lacking in another. The cost of comparison has a significant impact on women, more than you or I really want to admit. But we need to talk about it; we can't ignore our feelings any longer. This is how change begins.

Studies show that women suppress emotions and absorb the stress of others more than men do in order to maintain our roles in society. Dr. Gabor Maté, world renowned physician, speaker, and author, states that women have 80 percent of autoimmune disease because of greater stress, the tendency to suppress emotion, and more isolation. Science shows us that women are more risk-averse than men, as we are wired to take care of people around us, to be nurturing, and not to take on too much risk. An article in *Neuroscience & Biobehavioral Reviews* suggests that the evident differences in empathy between women and men could be due to gender and culture roles, as well as evolutionary and developmental influences. We are taught at a young age to play it safe; the message to be careful and not get hurt is ingrained in young girls, and as women we subconsciously take it with us into womanhood.

Men take on risk faster and more easily, and they do not focus on the implications of failure as heavily as women. Women tend to overprepare before we execute. We are scared to fail, and we tend to play it safe and strive to be perfect. It seems that men are more comfortable with uncertainty, and they trust that they will learn on the job, while women like to be prepared and strive for perfection.

The cost of waiting is at the expense of living.

Women wait for permission. We wait to be pretty enough, skinny enough, smart enough, financially secure enough, good enough, talented enough—to feel enough to do enough and to be enough. Waiting is weighing us all down. The cost of waiting is at the expense of living. When we wait, we put our life on hold and become passive witnesses rather than active participants in our own lives. When we wait for things to change, we miss living our lives.

In the book *The Confidence Code: The Science and Art of Self-Assurance—What Women Should Know*, Katty Kay and Claire Shipman break down the gap in confidence between men and women. They suggest that confidence is part science and part art. Their research shows that success correlates greater with confidence than competence, and yet women tend to focus on competence as they strive for perfection; women have lower overall self-confidence than men, and it shows up in many different aspects of life. The genetic blueprints of men and women are not extremely different for competence and confidence. Our mindsets make up the greatest differences.

Kay and Shipman write, "It isn't that women don't have the ability to succeed; it's that we don't seem to believe we *can* succeed, and that stops us from even trying." The real gender gap seems to arise not only from how we feel but also from how we respond to inevitable moments of self-doubt. Self-doubt is real for all of us, and becoming better at managing our insecurities—rather than our insecurities managing us—gives us confidence.

Kay and Shipman also point out a crucial difference between men and women when it comes to a lack of confidence: "We do a lot more ruminating than men." That can lead to analysis paralysis, while men often move into action. There are significant differences between how we think and what we think. Understanding these differences can help us lean into action without the need to feel confident before taking action.

Making change means stepping into the unfamiliar, which your brain does not like, even when the change is positive.

Neuroscience tells us that our limbic system is hardwired to prioritize safety and stability over risk. Subconsciously, our amygdala is constantly trying to assess the risk around us. That includes every thought we have and every action we're thinking about taking. Certainty always feels less risky than uncertainty, even if that uncertainty could lead us into a wonderful future. That message is reinforced all the time and communicated in common phrases such as "It's better to be safe than sorry." We don't want to lose our confidence, peace of mind, or reputation by making any kind of change.

This tendency toward certainty is more pronounced in women than in men. A paper from nonprofit research institute IZA demonstrates that women are more risk-averse than men, particularly in situations involving ambiguity. This study also explored how psychological traits might influence these differences in risk aversion and ambiguity aversion. It's not clear whether this is a biological difference or a social one, but we avoid risk.

Regardless, we are often taught as young girls to play it safe, even more so than young boys. "Be careful" and "Make sure you don't get hurt" are messages ingrained in us from a very early age, and these messages often carry over into adulthood.

This is normal. Our brains are wired first to prioritize the feeling of safety. We often feel safe in the certainty that's found by staying firmly in place. Staying stuck is one way that we have learned to be safe, because at least we know what to expect. We are programmed to think that change and uncertainty are not good for us, a message that is often passed down through the generations. But what if we could make change without feeling ready and be safe doing it? What if we could focus on lessening loss and being open to more gain as we change? Easier said than done, I know.

Waiting for More Time, Energy, and Money

I want to be real with you and let you know that I have done my share of waiting. In fact, I waited for more than ten years to feel ready to write this book. Ten whole years, waiting to have more time and more energy to do it, waiting for it to "feel right" and for me to "feel ready." I waited for over *one quarter of my life*.

But that feeling of readiness never did arrive. And it never does. Not on its own. You create it and make space for it, whatever your *it* may be.

The truth is I was stuck. I didn't have the slightest idea how to write a book. I couldn't even figure out what the first step should be. It didn't help that I had a learning disability in elementary school and was years behind my classmates in reading and writing. Even though I eventually caught up, it still sometimes shows up as a limiting belief.

But if I'm honest with myself, I was also afraid.

"What if I started it but couldn't finish? What would that say about me?"

"What if I finished, but it wasn't any good? What would *that* say about me?"

I knew I needed to develop some new skills, so I signed up for an online book workshop and met the most accomplished group of doctors, authors, leaders, speakers, and business owners and the very best writing coach, AJ Harper, from New York City. I was intimidated and did not feel ready to say the least, but a voice inside me said to go anyway.

On the last day of class, I put up my hand as I always did and asked a question of the group. "What gets in your way of doing what you really want to do?" I asked. I was in awe of these brilliant humans and wanted to test my philosophy on the brightest minds while I had direct access to them.

Their responses started flooding the Zoom chat:

Lack of time.

More lack of time.

Time, time, time.

These responses were automatic reactions that came out with no effort. I had assumed that money would not be an issue, due to their level of success, but time kept showing up.

Then I asked, "If I could give you twenty-four more hours a day, and it did not cost anything, what else would get in the way?"

The chat was silent. It became obvious that these professionals had probably never thought about this before. Perhaps you have never thought about this either. Then the real answers started to trickle in slowly, one at time.

The Harvard professor wrote first: "Not feeling ready or having enough credentials."

My jaw dropped.

The top salesperson for a massive multinational makeup company chimed in: "Not feeling ready, or who am I to do this?"

A sense of ease came over me as my book idea solidified. If top performers and leaders with doctorate degrees didn't feel ready, then this feeling clearly exists for everyone. No amount of success can make you feel ready for something you haven't yet tried.

We all want to feel ready before we do the thing we really want to do. We naturally disguise our hesitation as a lack of time and money because it's easier to justify those reasons. Limited resources are a real barrier for people, and even when they are not, we accept and understand those reasons whenever they are given.

But when we really think about what it would take for us to feel ready, if resources were not an issue, we get to the heart of the matter. Your fears show up disguised as a lack of time, lack of money, or some other logistical challenge. Really, it's the fear of embracing a new identity, fear of being seen, fear of failure, and fear of success, which are all about the big fear of change. We are all scared of change.

Telling ourselves that we are not ready gives us an excuse to stay stuck. We give a reason for why we have not done what we really want to do. Does this sound familiar to you?

As a girl with a learning disability, I was severely behind in reading and writing and struggling in school. Now I'm a woman who wrote a book. I'm an author. For me, that was one Big Freakin' Change and it wasn't easy. A BFC is a meaningful change, and it's harder than you could ever possibly imagine and also more rewarding than you could ever dream. You only get to experience it if you have the courage to pursue it, and yes, it may take more time than you ever imagined. But will it be worth it? Yes!

Just as I got over my own fears and took massive action and completed my course, factors outside my control came into play and knocked me down. My computer crashed one day after submitting my manuscript, leaving me without any of my research; my editor changed companies; and then my Los Angeles publisher closed up shop and I had to start the process again. OMG!! Trust me when I say I could have found a million reasons to give up, but I didn't want to live with regret, and I don't want you to either. BFCs often come with obstacles that you need to maneuver around.

What we need to know is that it's okay to not feel ready and to do it anyway. I want you to know the secret to reaching your goals is not as hard as you may think, and it is possible for you.

If you're feeling discontent in an area of your life, it's not a sign that something's necessarily wrong and it's not a sign that something within you is broken. It's a signal that something better is possible for you, that something better is *available to you* if you lean forward and take it. In fact, discontent is the birthplace of many dreams. Just like the inner voices of fear and self-criticism, discontent can actually provide us with wonderful insight if we have the courage to listen.

Yet most of us just stay stuck, unable to step toward that dream and make the changes we want. We think we need to have confidence before we take action, so we stay waiting and stay stuck. It's okay to acknowledge you're stuck and that you want more out of life and then give yourself permission to make change.

But many of us won't change because we tend to *over*estimate the challenges facing us and *under*estimate all of the ways that our life has prepared us for this particular moment. We are so often stronger, wiser, and more capable than we give ourselves credit for. Massive growth happens through the challenges and changes we experience in life.

Big Freakin' Change

Some changes happen without any input from us at all. These are the changes that happen to us and are largely unavoidable. Others happen with ease, requiring only minimal effort on our part. But the changes I'm most interested in for you, and for myself, are the changes that light a spark *within* us. You know the ones I'm talking about. This is the change that occupies your mind during the day and keeps you awake at night. This is the change that scares your panties off and inspires you to put your big girl panties on. This is the change that speaks to the depth of your soul and makes you question whether or not you have what it takes to make it. These are the changes that can make a significant impact not only on your life but also on the lives of many others.

This is what I call your BFC, your Big Freakin' Change: *significant, pivotal, life-defining, monumental change* that promises to not only change your circumstances but also to change *you* in the process. The change you avoid, and the change you know you need to make. This book is about making that kind of change—a BFC.

If only you knew how to make it right. If only you weren't too scared to take the first and then the second and even the third step. If only you could find the confidence, the clarity, and the courage to make it. If only you knew *how* to make the change.

Every BFC has the potential to serve as a picture frozen in time marking the before and after moment for you, a change so significant that it defines a pivotal era of your life for the rest of your life. A BFC provides you with the perspective of "That was then, and this is now."

A BFC may be taking that gap year to travel, which changes your perspective on the world and ends up shifting your career path. Perhaps your BFC is starting that first business in your "free" time, which increases your appetite for risk and you start to play bigger. Your BFC may be ending that relationship, which gives you the space to see the pattern you kept repeating and allows you to show up in your next relationship as a healthier version of yourself.

Although it can be hard to determine which changes will have that kind of impact in advance, our intuitive minds drop hints all the time. In my experience, these show up as daydreams in our quiet moments. When our minds are left to dance in an open space or play on the playground of possibility, pay very close attention to the moves they make. These kinds of changes also show up as whispers trying to get your attention or repeated thoughts that surface. They will pull on your heart, occupy your mind, and are available for the taking... if, and only if, you have the courage to listen.

I encourage you to pay attention before your rational mind makes a counteroffer; it's rarely as exciting and is usually just more of the same of your status quo. More of the same doesn't require you to do anything different or make any change. It certainly doesn't require you to *be* anything different. And that's the problem. In order to make a pivotal change in our lives, we need to step into a new identity, the next version of ourselves. When there is discomfort and a change requires us to see ourselves differently, that's a clue that we're on the right track.

These are the kind of changes you see in before and after pictures. "I used to be... but now I am..."

These are the kind of changes that are so big that we can look back and see a clear line drawn in the sand of our timeline. And these are the kinds of changes that also make us feel stuck before we make them. Being stuck is a gift: it tells you something better is available for you.

BFCs are not easy to make or insignificant. They are the changes that scare you but that also inspire you. They are the changes that, if made, will have a ripple effect throughout the rest of your life. They have the potential to shift the way you see yourself and the way you see the world around you. They are the kinds of changes that straddle the intersection of hope and disbelief, fear and courage, possibility and problems, and stress and success. These are the changes no one likes to talk about and few have the courage to make. A BFC can set your life in motion and give you momentum like never before.

And just a heads-up, when we activate our courage and take action, people around us will have opinions. Remember that other people's judgments often stem from their own insecurities and are not a reflection of you. It's not a reason to back down; use it as fuel to push forward. Most people play it safe in life and avoid making BFCs... but not you!

So what's the Big Freakin' Change that you want to make right now?

Maybe you immediately know what it is. Perhaps you picked up this book with the hope of finding the courage, the stamina, the motivation, the process to finally step into it. Or it could be that you know you need to make a change, but you're not entirely sure what that change is. Either way you are right where you need to be. Here, now. Reading and learning about how to make your BFC.

When the Stakes Are High, We Wait Longer

A BFC is a significant change, which is why you are stuck waiting. When the stakes are high and the BFC will cause a significant change in our identity, we want to feel ready that much more and we wait that much longer. Sometimes change is thrown in our face and breaks us into pieces, and we have to build ourselves back up. Regardless of the change you are experiencing—a relationship, career, or identity change—when you stop waiting to feel ready, you experience change.

Take Mary, for example.

Mary is a hardworking, ambitious professional woman in her thirties with big dreams to grow her marketing business and travel the world. She worked hard for her career and has a wonderful husband; she has the freedom and the flexibility to create her own reality but notices she wants more in her life. She has decided she wants to start a family. Though she's unsure of how she will balance her professional career with motherhood, she takes a leap of faith and decides to start a family. Her identity will change forever.

And Claudia.

Claudia is a hardworking single mom with two young daughters, hustling to make ends meet. Her work never escapes her mind; her job is sucking her soul. She wants to leave her corporate job and start her dream job. She knows she needs to make a change but doesn't feel ready. She is stuck in analysis paralysis, unsure how to make a move. She decides not to take action until she has more money saved.

Or Darlene.

Darlene just turned sixty, beginning a new decade and chapter in her life. She woke up one morning and looked at herself hard in the mirror, as if she was seeing herself for the first time in years. She had an emptiness inside her heart that she could no longer cover up with her clothes or makeup. Her heart was heavy, carrying all the heartache

Telling ourselves that we are not ready **gives us an excuse to stay stuck.**

from her broken marriage. She decided to leave her marriage and redesign her life after a decade of waiting for things to change. She wanted to feel ready, but when readiness never came to her, she realized it wasn't coming and instead she had to act.

What happened to them, and what happens to most of us, is that when we are faced with a decision to make a significant change that will alter our identity, we wait to feel ready without really understanding what exactly is holding us back. We are scared to let go of who we are and step into who we will become. We have blind spots and believe we need more time, energy, or money; we justify it by thinking that it's just not the right time. What we may not realize is that with all the waiting, we are not being true to ourselves, and we lose ourselves one piece at a time. Our hopes, our dreams, and our identity. We can all find a million reasons not to make a change, but I encourage you to find one reason to do it. What will be your reason?

Making change changes you, and you simply can't prepare for that. Your thoughts, habits, behaviors, and desires will also change. Friction and fear are part of the molding process of transformation—the process of evolving into the next version of ourselves. I want you to know that being stuck is not a problem; it is simply a sign that you are entering a transitional phase in life, and you desire more and are capable of more. Being stuck is your cue to move and make a BFC. Just by choosing to pick up this book, you have started to break the cycle of waiting. You took action. You don't need to procrastinate any longer, and you don't need to make change perfectly. You just need to make a move and take the next right step.

The Real Reason We Don't Make a BFC

I've had conversations with thousands of women over the years about making BFCs and a common theme has emerged. *We just don't feel ready.* But we think we would feel ready if we only had more time, more energy, or more money. All three of those—or rather the lack of them—are legitimate barriers to making BFCs. Of course they are. But in my experience, they are more often than not simply fear dressed up as a reasonable excuse for inaction. It's hard to make intentional changes, let alone BFCs.

The secret realization that unlocks our ability to make those BFCs anyway is that readiness is not a state of being but a feeling that comes after you take action.

Let me say that again...

Readiness is *not* a state of being but a feeling that comes *after* you take action. The feeling of readiness before we make a new change, especially a BFC, does not exist, so we must stop waiting to feel ready. Once you take action, you will feel ready. It doesn't happen before. You can do things without feeling ready. It's okay to be unready.

It's by *starting* that we find ourselves on the path to making our BFCs, and only then do we find the confidence to keep going. Confidence comes after we make change, not before. We develop our confidence through taking action.

Our understanding of confidence is backward. We always assume that we must *feel* confident before we make a change in our lives, but it's the complete opposite. Take action first and confidence will follow. The model of confidence is backward. I will show you why so that you can take the next step forward and develop your confidence along the way. This is good news because change is easier than you think and nothing is wrong with you, but the way we view confidence is wrong.

Taking a step forward when we don't feel ready requires courage, and even more courage when we feel perfectly *unready*. But once we take action, we will gain clarity, and that clarity will give us confidence. It's self-reinforcing and builds our confidence over time. All types of change start with courage. Picking up this book proved that you are courageous, and that change is possible. You just need to learn how to make change, and this book will teach you the steps involved.

The Backward Confidence Model

When we say we are waiting to feel ready before we do something, what this *really* means is that we are waiting to feel confident. We need to stop waiting to feel ready or confident before we act.

The truth is we may never get to *ready*. We can prepare for sure, but think about it, our entire lives we are asked if we are ready. Are you ready for school, ready to get married, ready to have a baby… the list goes on. That is the problem. We need to stop asking people if they are ready to do something they have never done before.

You are not the problem, and your lack of confidence is not the issue. The model of confidence we have in society is backward. Rediscovering how confidence is created gives us a new lens to see our lives and make decisions that serve us. Change is easier than you think once you understand how confidence is developed.

This is how we currently think about confidence.

HOW PEOPLE CURRENTLY THINK ABOUT CONFIDENCE

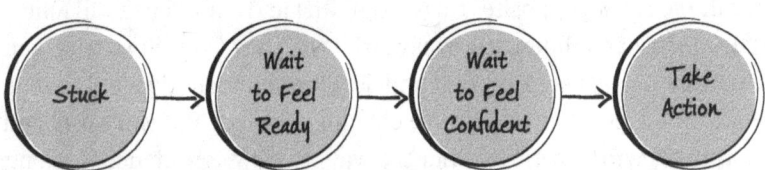

We feel stuck and want to take action, but we wait to feel ready so we can feel confident enough to take action. But readiness doesn't exist, so we remain stuck.

Here is how confidence is *actually* created!

REAL CONFIDENCE MODEL

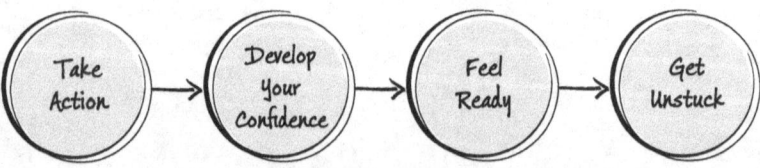

In the real confidence model, we flip the coin. We *start* by taking action, which develops our confidence, and that confidence makes us feel ready. This process helps us get unstuck. If you are like me, I know you want to get unstuck first, but the reality is you get unstuck last.

Instead of waiting for someone—a mentor, coach, spouse, parent, friend, or boss—to tap us on the shoulder and say, "You're ready," we must step out onto the stage of life so we can feel ready.

Now, I know I'm making this process sound simple. I acknowledge it's not. This is why I created the Get Unstuck, Cycle of Change Model that I will share in the next chapter; it will help you move through the change you've been wanting to make. It's by *starting* that we find ourselves on the path to our BFCs, and only then do we find the confidence to keep going.

Your Next Chapter

Of course, you have the option to choose to do nothing, and nothing in your life will change and you can choose to live with regret. But who wants that?! I hope that you know you are worthy, loved, and so deserving of your desires now. Just as you are today. You don't need to wait any longer. Bestselling author of *Worthy* and *Believe It* Jamie Kern Lima writes, "Self-confidence is the belief in your abilities as a person... Self-worth is the belief in your value as a person." You are already proven valuable just by being alive. You beat the odds. Just being born is a chance of 1 in 400 trillion. So, embrace that you are already worthy of your desires, and build your confidence to do great things. Find your courage, experience clarity, and develop your confidence. There are no shortcuts, but I promise it will be worth it.

Confidence looks different on everyone, but it feels the same on the inside. It's not about having perfect posture, smiling all the time, speaking eloquently, being successful, or having lots of money. Confidence is the feeling of no longer comparing yourself to others. It's giving yourself permission to take up space, and it's the ability to be seen and accepted for who you are, knowing you are fully worthy as you are right now. It's belonging to yourself, and it's the energy that you emanate regardless of who is around you or the challenges that surround you. It's about stepping out of the wings when you don't feel ready and knowing you can trust yourself. When you do this, you transform into a beacon of light, hope, and inspiration for others to do the same.

Confidence is also about no longer tolerating things that are not in alignment with your values and vision for your life. It's about using your voice, protecting your values, and celebrating your vision for your life. It's a sense of inner peace from the knowledge that you will find your way even when it's challenging. Confidence has been defined as "a feeling of self-assurance arising from one's appreciation of one's own abilities or qualities." It is developed over time by getting positive outcomes. If you don't try, you won't discover the abilities and qualities you already have waiting to be developed.

Making a BFC is a lot like dance. There are many steps along the way. Some people will feel uncomfortable doing it, and for others, it will totally be your jam, making you feel like a superstar. You will travel forward and at times need to take steps back and try again. You will feel lost until you find your beat with your feet. Making a BFC is like doing the cha-cha: awkward until you find your rhythm. Then you will gain momentum and be on fire. So get excited to move and make change.

If you already know the change you want to make, then I'm excited for you. You are about to make some major progress, and you will change yourself in the process. There is so much that is possible for you that you can't even comprehend yet! If you are still searching to know what change is required, I am thrilled for you. You get to write the next chapter of your life.

I promise that by the end of this book, you will have increased confidence, and you'll be able to take the next right step and stop waiting. This is your invitation to get unstuck. My dream for you is that if you do the work, you will take center stage in your own life.

Hand on Heart

One thing about me is that I feel things deeply, I think about things strategically, and I like to prepare my mind, body, and soul for decisions in life, especially when making big changes. Through years of experience, I have personally received huge clarity and direction by doing this hand on heart exercise every morning before my feet hit the ground, which is why I want to share it with you. I have also taught thousands of girls as young as age six and women as wise as seventy this little exercise to tap into inner peace when they are feeling disconnected. If you think you are too busy for this or not feeling up to it, this is especially for you. When you are in the midst of change, your mind, body, and soul are often disconnected. Bringing them back together in unity will provide you with the clarity and courage to move forward and develop your confidence.

So go ahead and place your hand on your heart and take a few deep breaths in and out slowly. Pay attention to your breath and see if you can slow down and deepen your breathing. Drop your shoulders. Let your tongue melt from the roof of your mouth to the bottom, and take a moment just to be. Be here for yourself fully as you are.

Repeat this affirmation:

It is okay to make changes in my life. I give myself permission to change and create a life that I love.

Now ask yourself these questions and see what comes up for you:

What is the change I want to make?

What am I really scared of?

When I was courageous in the past, how did that feel?

Repeat this statement:

I have everything I need inside of me to make the change I desire. I need to tap into my courage to build my confidence. It's okay to take a chance to make a change. I am giving myself permission to expand into the next version of myself.

P.S. You've got this.

2
COURAGE TO CHANGE

*"Grant me the serenity to accept the things
I cannot change, the courage to change the things I can,
and the wisdom to know the difference."*

REINHOLD NIEBUHR

WHEN I WAS TWENTY in New York City dancing at the Broadway Dance Center for a summer, I learned about an audition for a television commercial in Calgary, where I live, on the day I would be flying home. They were looking for someone to dance to Britney Spears and lip sync. I would not be home in time, but I loved Britney Spears back in the day and had always dreamed of being in commercials. There was a part of me that always trusted myself while another part of me thought I was crazy to even dream this big and sat in fear. This is why most of us get stuck and stay stuck: we have a battle between our dreams and our reality. Courage is the bridge that connects them.

Maybe you thought you were the only one feeling stuck, but you're not alone. In fact, a study by Oracle and Workplace Intelligence suggests that over 75 percent of people feel "stuck" personally and professionally. We need a pathway to change to help us get unstuck.

An article in *Forbes* states that "autonomy [is] critical to people's wellbeing, happiness and mental health ... When people feel empowered to make their own decisions, they are usually happier with the outcomes and more engaged." We need to acknowledge we feel stuck so we can get unstuck and make necessary change to improve our well-being.

A study published in the *Quarterly Journal of Economics* reports that close to 80 percent of women struggle with low self-esteem. It's time for change. You don't need to feel confident: you need courage.

Back to the audition. Instead of disqualifying myself because the logistics did not work, I tapped into my courage and emailed the casting agency my headshot and résumé. I told them I felt the job was for me and I asked if it would be possible to fit me in later in the day. I knew it was a big ask; I didn't even have an agent at that time and was unsure if they would consider me. To my delight, they agreed!

On my way home, my connecting flight was delayed and my luggage was lost; I would not make the late audition time that they had graciously agreed to. I could have just called them and said I could not make it, but my intuition told me to pause. I put my hand on my heart and asked, "Cara, do you want this job?" *Yes.*

"Cara, what is the worst thing that can happen?" *They say no.*

"Can you live with that answer?" *Hell yes.*

"Make the call," I said to myself.

I took a deep breath and reminded myself to feel my feet on the floor, grounding myself. "Just tap into your courage, Cara, and see what happens," I whispered to myself. Ever since I was a young girl, I always felt like I knew who I was in my soul. This has served me well in life, as I can tap into my soul before making big decisions.

I went to the payphone and inserted my coins into the slot. As each one dropped in, I fell further and further into the second-guessing game. I pulled out the number that I had written on a Juicy Fruit gum wrapper and dialed, my heart pounding. I reminded myself to breathe, process the emotion of fear, and still move forward with my highest intention of love.

"Hello, this is Cara. I have an audition tonight at seven o'clock, which I was kindly provided with. I'm so sorry, but my plane has been delayed tonight," I said with the airport announcements echoing loudly in the background.

I took a deep breath and closed my eyes, gathering every bit of courage I had in myself while thinking, "Who the heck does this and who the heck do I think I am?"

"Is there any possible way you could bump my time back even further?"

I was met with silence on the phone, and the lady exhaled deeply. My heart began racing.

"No one has ever been as persistent as you've been, so I guess I will give you a shot."

I thanked her profusely as I hung up the phone and fist-pumped the air as hard as I could. Wow, I asked, and they said yes!

On my way from Toronto to Calgary, I stressed over showing up at the audition in my unflattering traveling outfit, late, and not looking my best. In the world of auditioning, your appearance is always taken into account. You want to show up and shine. My insecurities came creeping in, knowing there would be other women auditioning who were prettier, more polished, and more trained than me.

"Don't worry about all of the external noise. Trust, Cara," I told myself. "Trust yourself. You've got this."

I landed in Calgary, and my amazing mom came to the rescue, as she always did. She picked me up, lost luggage nowhere to be found on the carousel, and we went straight to the agency downtown. She could tell I was a bit nervous and reminded me, "Just try your best and let go of the rest." She always would remind me to just be myself. In a world where expectations are high, we sometimes need to calm down and remember to just be ourselves.

I walked into the skyscraper downtown and took the elevator up to the third floor, my heartbeat loud in my ears. As the nerves washed over me, I stood there, focusing on taking deep breaths and reminding myself how excited I was for this experience. I stepped out of the elevator and took a seat in the empty waiting room.

A lady came out and called my name. I walked in with my heart open and head up. "I am a little hot and sweaty, I did not even have powder to put on my face, my luggage was lost, I am late but I am grateful. Thank you for giving me this opportunity."

I pulled my hair back into a tight ponytail, turned around to the back of the room, and hit a sharp pose. I was sure they would have me dance to one of Britney Spears's top hits, "... Baby One More Time" or "Crazy."

Nope!

They played a different song: "I Will Be There." I couldn't believe it. *Oh my god*. My heartbeat returned to my ears, threatening to drown everything out. "Trust, Cara, trust. You made it this far. Don't give up now," the voice inside me whispered. "You are ready to show them what you got."

I danced my heart out, turning my head away from the casting directors when I was unsure of the words, and gave it all I had. I hit a pose when the song ended and smiled. Out of breath, panting, and embarrassed about not knowing the lyrics, I cautiously asked, "Was that what you were looking for?"

I looked at the two men and one woman, trying to read their body language. One man smiled, and the other two looked at each other with no emotion at all. I tried my best to silence my heavy breathing and kept smiling and making eye contact, standing tall with my shoulders back. I was hot and sweaty and full of my belief in the possibility but standing with the reality of fear.

The casting director finally said, "We appreciate your determination and persistence, and that was enough to give you an audition."

Silence again. I started to get sweatier as my self-doubt returned. "Oh my god, I did not get the job," I thought.

Then the casting manager said, "That was awesome. You are exactly what we are looking for and have so much energy."

I beamed and thanked them as I shook their hands and walked as calmly as I could back into the elevator while I screamed on the inside. "Yes!" Nothing had worked in my favor, but I had the courage to ask for the audition, the courage to show up, and the courage to try my best despite the challenges. I then had confidence after I got the job.

After shooting the first commercial, Jim, the cameraperson, said, "Cara, I got to give it to you. You are completely open to feedback and want to do a good job. You are easy to work with, and we appreciate that about you."

I think what he was really noticing was that I was comfortable with myself and trusted myself to try new things. That job led to two more television commercials without an audition process, which never happens in the entertainment industry. I showed up and did my best. I listened to my feelings, trusted myself, had the courage to ask and the courage to step out even when I was clearly not ready. When you can imagine it, you can create it. You just need to take the first step and push fear aside. Step into courage.

The Procrastination and Perfectionism Loop

Being stuck shows up in different ways; we are all stuck some of the time. I was not ready at all to audition for the commercial. Heck, I was not even in the same country, was not represented by an agent, and didn't have dance shoes on. But I went for it because I believed in myself and my potential, and I was okay with rejection. When we focus on all the reasons we are not ready, we often avoid taking a chance on ourselves, and we procrastinate, striving for perfection. Think about all of the things you wanted to do but didn't; instead, you kept waiting to feel ready. Well, my friend, this is procrastination at its finest and perfectionism in disguise.

Before we enter change, we usually experience procrastination or perfectionism. We can get overwhelmed and decide to procrastinate, or we find ourselves overpreparing as we strive for perfection. In both cases, we never take action. When we let go of perfectionism, we can get ahead of procrastination and take action.

Ellen Taaffe, professor and director of women's leadership at the Kellogg School of Management and author of *The Mirrored Door*, explains why women with great potential get trapped in a cycle of what she defines as "preparing to perfection": "Women encounter the 'mirrored door' at some point in our careers—the place where, when presented with opportunities, we reflect inward and hesitate, and deem we're not ready or worthy enough to move forward, whether that is to raise our hands or go for the next role." Taaffe writes, "Too many well-equipped women reflect inward and hesitate or procrastinate instead of risking action."

Even if we know we could transform into something more magnificent, we choose routine and consistency because that is all we know, and our brains are prediction machines. In fear of making a mistake, we overprepare and strive for perfection, or we avoid and procrastinate as overwhelming feelings wash over us when we think about change. Both are a kind of tug-of-war we play within ourselves. Perfectionism and procrastination are two sides of the same coin.

Accept the change and move forward.

Perfectionism and procrastination are two sides of the same coin. **Accept the change and move forward.**

Embrace Your Fear

Often, we don't take action because we're afraid: afraid of the unknown, of failure, of discomfort, or even of being judged by others. But when we take that first step into courage, it brings us to clarity. Clarity helps us develop our confidence and initiate momentum toward our BFCs.

Movement brings us into a new perspective. Each new perspective helps us find clarity that we didn't have before. But often we want to see the entire path before taking the first step.

With courage and clarity in our back pockets, the lack of confidence that felt so powerful before is not quite so important anymore. It turns out that we've been underestimating ourselves all along because the model of confidence we have is backward.

I was coming from New York City where the dance talent was unbelievable. I was a small fish in a big pond. I was drowning trying to stay afloat. I was afraid when I asked for that audition time and afraid when I asked to reschedule. Yet I walked alongside the fear because I had courage. This is what courage does for us. It helps us make change one step at a time even when we don't feel ready or fully prepared. Just like you, I thought that I should feel confident before going after what I really wanted, in this case the audition. But this is the problem: we can't feel confident before doing something we have not done before. Just acknowledging that you are stuck in your life right now, feeling disconnected or unfulfilled, will help you navigate change. The first step in the Get Unstuck, Cycle of Change Model is to acknowledge you're stuck.

Understanding Change

Change is inevitable and yet we avoid it out of fear.

I want to tell you about my badass friend who I thought had no fear. I've known Shaima since university. I've always admired her sense of adventure and her joie de vivre. It was well known in our circle of friends that if you wanted someone to do something crazy with, Shaima was your girl. There was nothing she wouldn't try. She was the last person you would expect to ever feel stuck. Yet here she was in front of me looking as if life had kicked the wind out of her and she couldn't find her breath.

"I don't even *recognize* myself anymore," Shaima choked out to me between tears. "I used to be so excited about my life. But now…" She paused and closed her eyes as if waiting for the right words. "Now… I just feel *stuck*. I feel *stuck*."

"What's going on, girl?" I asked her, my heart heavy for my friend.

"That's the thing, Cara. I'm not really sure. It's nothing really. My life is good. I keep being promoted at work. My relationship with my boyfriend isn't perfect, but it's the best one I've ever had. I've got decent savings in the bank and can afford pretty much anything I want. But still… I know I am made for more. There's a part of me that just wants to blow everything up and start again. I don't know. I just feel like I'm not living *my* life; I'm living a life that was designed for someone else. I wanted to have *adventure*, and I'm stuck in this boring life, going through the motions. Every day feels like a repeat of the day before. I wanted *more* from my life. I *want* more from my life. But I don't know what I should do, or if change is even possible."

Normally a very confident woman, Shaima visibly shrunk before my eyes as she explained how she felt. She felt trapped in a life that was too small and too safe to match the fire she had in her belly.

What Shaima didn't know in that moment was how deeply I could relate to what she was feeling. It didn't look like it from the outside, but man, could I feel it on the inside. I felt so stuck. It's a feeling no one wants to talk about. It's uncomfortable and foreign for most of us.

Generations of women were rarely encouraged to make change. When I take a moment to think about where I came from, I'm thankful to my mom, my aunts, my grandmothers, and my great-grandmothers for the many ways they paved the way for the life I get to live today. Because of them and the women of their generations, life as a woman is so much easier for me than it was for them. I have more opportunities than they ever dreamed of. And I want my daughter, Claire, to have more opportunities than I've ever dreamed of. I want her to grow up and be surrounded by women who are living out loud from the center of their brilliance. Women who live without needing permission, who feel like they are enough, and who don't apologize for being too much (a criticism that only ever seems to be directed at women who live large). Think about the generations of women you came from, and perhaps you can find gratitude and dream bigger for the generations that come after you.

In Shaima's case, she came from women who were the opposite of her: they had played it safe and small. Shaima dreamed big and wanted more, which is something I love about her. She knew that she wanted to make a change in her life, but she didn't know what it was. She didn't have clarity, and she couldn't find the confidence to make a change. Her inner critic kept telling her she had plenty and should be content. But something deep down inside of her wanted to make change, and my guess is that it's the same for you.

Shaima felt stuck in life and needed to make a change. I was stuck with obstacles stacked against me with my commercial audition. In both cases, we tapped into our courage to move forward. Shaima took time off from her accounting job and followed her passion to be a fitness and yoga instructor with courage. I drew on my courage to put myself out there, which landed me three commercials, music videos, and some modeling opportunities.

Give yourself some grace; you may not have all of the answers now. But when you look back on your life, you'll see in hindsight how the dots connect. Start with courage, and your confidence will come. Put your inner critic aside.

Have you ever been talked out of making a big change by your inner critic? You might expect me to tell you to ignore that voice, especially when it appears to be a barrier to actually making change. But how has that worked for you so far? What happens when you don't listen to that inner voice? Does it get quieter? Does it go away? Or does it get louder and louder, eventually yelling at you until you pay attention? For me, it's the latter.

Instead of being the enemy of change, those voices help us to see the doorway to it. It's important to realize that each time we hear the voice of fear, of our inner critic, we are being given information by our subconscious. Sometimes that information is simply "I'm afraid." That's it. Other times, the voice gives us valuable guidelines for how to make a change. You can go as fast or slow as you like, but you need to go through the cycle, step by step.

When I asked bestselling author of *Big Magic* Elizabeth Gilbert what to do when we are stuck in life and want to make change, she shared an interesting point of view: "If you are feeling stuck, you are not lost; you couldn't be if you tried." She shared that small curiosities help us move forward; following tiny little pebbles helps us move forward and encourages us to stop looking for the big things. I couldn't agree more. Small steps lead to massive change, but most of us wait for the big things in our life to change before we tap into our courage to make change.

Most of us stay stuck, unable to step toward our dream. It's okay to acknowledge that you're stuck and want more out of your life and to give yourself permission to make change. But what comes next? The Get Unstuck, Cycle of Change Model is the easiest way I know to make a BFC. So, while nothing worthwhile is accomplished without any effort, you may be surprised at how much easier it is to make the change than you expect.

The Get Unstuck, Cycle of Change Model shows you what to expect and the steps involved.

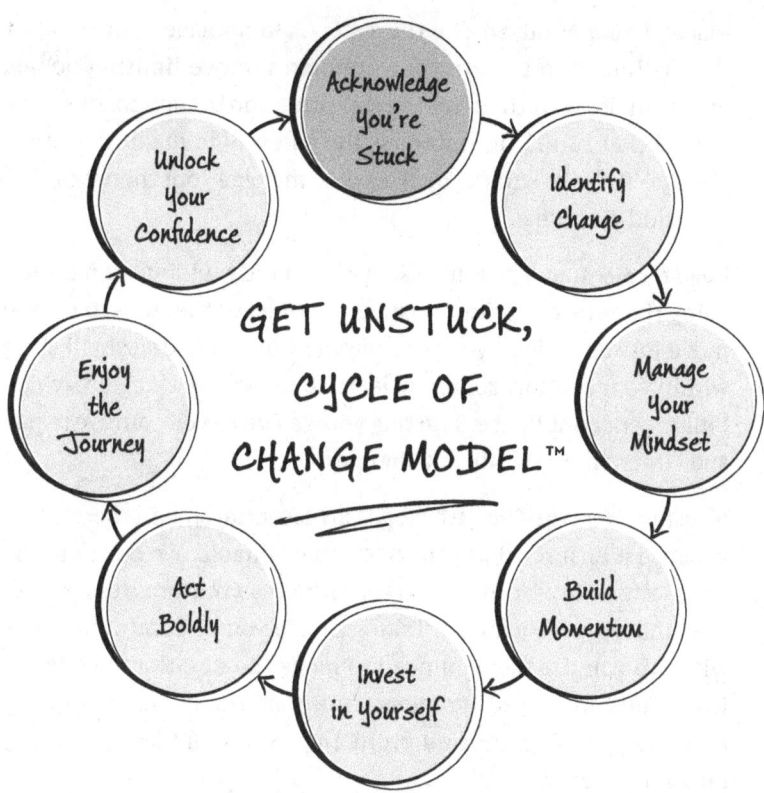

1. **Acknowledge You're Stuck:** The first step is to acknowledge and accept that you are stuck. We can never change what we don't acknowledge. Examine your feelings, your inner critic, and your desires, and take time to be curious about what your life could look like.

2. **Identify Change:** The second step is to identify the specific change we'd like to make. Often, we carry around a vague idea of something we'd like to alter. The idea of change can be so amorphous that it gives us nothing to hold on to. Take time to identify the part of your life that feels off and get clear on the adjustment you want to make. This may include physical, intellectual, emotional, social, spiritual, vocational, financial, and environmental dimensions of change.

3. **Manage Your Mindset:** The third step is to manage your mindset. You will need to update your outlook, remove limiting beliefs, and evaluate your thoughts. Paying attention to the subconscious stories that run in our minds is the gateway to making positive change. To make a BFC, you'll learn to manage your thoughts, feelings, and emotions.

4. **Build Momentum:** The fourth step is all about building momentum using the zone of optimal change. You'll learn the steps to take to move forward. When you build momentum by taking small steps within your comfort zone, you learn to trust yourself again, which builds your confidence. Trusting yourself gives you courage to pursue larger, more significant changes.

5. **Invest in Yourself:** The fifth step is an essential step in the process because it ensures that your BFC is sustainable. We'll look at the right way to invest in rest so that it helps your progress, rather than moves you backward. Taking care of yourself and your needs will give you the fuel you need to make the BFC that you desire. Investing in yourself includes resting mentally and physically, reflecting on your life, and protecting your boundaries to maintain your energy.

6. **Act Boldly:** The sixth step is all about forming a new relationship with fear so you can act boldly and move forward. This is the most important step in making a BFC. You'll learn how fear can actually be an ally, not an enemy, in helping you to make your BFC. Embracing your fear is required to step outside your comfort zone and meet the next version of yourself.

7. **Enjoy the Journey:** The seventh step is about finding joy in your journey. Joy is always a choice. Joyfulness reinforces the changes that we are making and reminds us of who we are and what we want in life. When you approach your BFC, your landscape for possibilities expands and you discover what else is possible. You may not feel the way you anticipated before you made the change, because you've changed. Happiness is temporary; joy is longer

lasting. Happiness often stems from accomplishment; joy is more of a state of being. Happiness is connected to doing; joy is connected to being.

8. **Unlock Your Confidence:** The eighth step is both an acknowledgment of the process thus far and an invitation to let it sink into the deepest cracks of your being. You'll have grown in confidence along the way, and you can learn to feed your confidence so that it's stronger the next time you want to make a BFC. When you enter into your next change, you'll do so with your unlocked level of confidence and this time you'll also know the framework to navigate change. Each time you embrace change, your tolerance for it increases, as does your resiliency. You'll discover what you're made of and step into your brilliance. This is the most exciting stage as you inspire others to do the same.

The Get Unstuck, Cycle of Change Model works if you work it. By picking up this book and reading these first chapters, you've already completed step one. Let's be real: unless you'd acknowledged that you want to make a change in your life, you would never read a book on how to do just that. So give yourself a high five and remind yourself that you will never feel ready. You just need to give yourself permission to go.

You probably thought this was another how-to book. It's more of a permission-to book. Of course, you will get lots of tools and a framework in here too, so that you can make your BFC. This is your invitation and opportunity to make the change you want.

My biggest hope for you is that as you walk through this model, you'll realize how powerful you actually are. And that you will give yourself the permission you need to walk boldly into your most beautiful future with confidence. It's time to step into your brilliance and become the next version of yourself. You were made for greatness.

Boom! Let's go!

Hand on Heart

I invite you to take a moment to connect with yourself.

Take a moment to lie down and close your eyes. Connect to your feelings. Place your hand on your heart, and connect with your breath. Breathe. Feel your hand on your body, and pay attention to your breath, and see if you can feel your heartbeat. Invite yourself to reconnect with your body, heart, and mind.

Ask yourself what you want and just listen to your voice and intuition. Pay attention.

Whatever comes to mind, keep asking yourself, "Why?" The answer will arrive. Eyes closed, and hand on heart.

P.S. It's okay to feel stuck in the messy middle.
You will get out of the muck by taking one step at a time.
You'll learn how to do just this.

3 TYPES OF CHANGE

"The only way to make sense out of change is to plunge into it, move with it, and join the dance."

ALAN WATTS

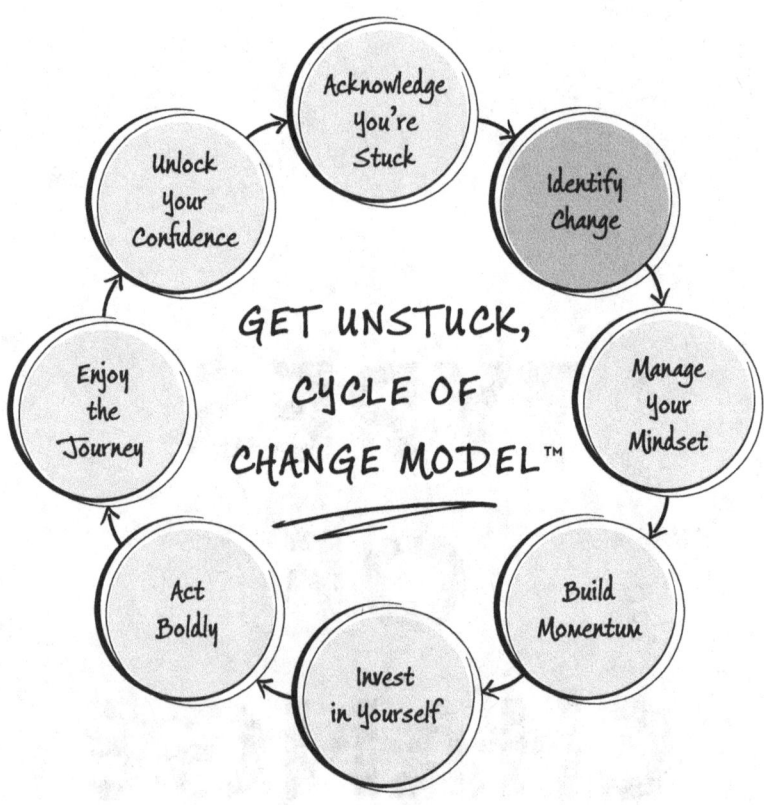

Now that you have identified that you are stuck, we'll explore the type of change you want to experience. Once you clearly identify it, it feels easier to navigate.

IN 2019, I ATTENDED a dance industry conference in New York City with my besties, Amanda and Courtney. We all own thriving studios and take advantage of every opportunity to be with each other; conferences like this one provide the perfect excuse.

Amazing things always seem to happen when we're together: we get invited to special parties, receive free upgrades at hotels, get free tickets to concerts, and people come up to us to tell us there's "something about you ladies." It's happened so many times that we started calling ourselves "The Power of Three."

We have a really deep heart connection. We see each other for exactly who we are and give ourselves permission to be seen. No one of us outshines the others, and no one of us holds back. We're not only there for the good times. When one of us is going through a hard time, the others hold space and bring light and love in. We've developed so much love and trust with each other over the years that it's hard to imagine what my life would be without them. Friends like these are true gifts for the soul.

Anyway, after our conference wrapped up, Courtney and I decided to stop in at Macy's for a little shopping spree. I love fashion, but I love a great deal on fashion even more.

As we cruised up and down floors and through different aisles, I ran my fingers over the different textures of the clothing. I found a pretty red scoop-neck top on sale and held it up. "Do you like this one?" I asked Courtney. "You would look good in this!"

She furrowed her eyebrows. "No, not really."

"What about this one?" I asked, pulling up a gorgeous royal-blue blouse.

"Nah, it's not really my style."

"Okay," I said. "What about this black blazer?"

Courtney shifted awkwardly, staring intently at an object on the floor only visible to her. "I..." She paused. "I don't really feel like shopping for clothes anymore, Cara."

She looked up at me cautiously, as if assessing if it was okay in this moment to be vulnerable.

"It's not that I don't feel like shopping, actually. It's just that nothing on this floor will fit me."

I paused, then said, "Well, let's go to the floor that has clothes that fit you."

She froze and pursed her lips, visibly conflicted. She had never imagined herself in the plus-sized section before. Shopping there would mean accepting her reality. In this one area, she was stuck in the past, and it was holding her back from looking and feeling her best.

Like many women, Courtney was waiting until she lost weight to buy new clothes and did not even *consider* investing in herself until she did. She didn't feel ready. She wanted to be on the diet, do all the exercises, and lose weight, so she could gain back her self-acceptance and confidence. Each day she was sure it was the day to start, but life happened, and she never found the time or had enough energy to start making the big changes she wanted. She made lists of recipes to make, exercises to do, and diet hacks to try. The lists of things to do were piling up. They were becoming obstacles and obligations she needed to overcome rather than resources to support her. She was feeling more uncomfortable with her physical appearance. The disconnect she felt was no longer tolerable, and it was bleeding into other areas of her life.

This left her stuck shopping on the wrong floor for years, feeling crappy about herself every single time. In her heart, she wanted to look great and feel confident in her clothes and more importantly in her skin. Years of self-judgment had slowly chipped away at her belief that it was even possible. She lost her hope without even realizing it. She just stayed waiting. She was waiting to lose the extra weight before she would do things she wanted: travel, buy new clothes, plan parties, and live more fully. Her weight was increasing rather than decreasing, despite her greatest efforts. Under all the stress-inducing lists and plans, she was waiting to feel worthy again without being aware of what was really standing in her way. As her weight increased, her perception of her worth decreased.

Like so many of us, Courtney squeezed herself into clothes that didn't fit her anymore. But she was also trying to squeeze herself into a past that didn't fit anymore, into old beliefs and expectations that didn't fit anymore. It wasn't only about the clothes. They were just the visible expression of what was going on inside her.

Sensing that, I wanted to help her see what was possible and rediscover the inherent worthiness that was always there, even if she couldn't feel it at that moment.

As we went up the escalator to the floor with plus-sized clothes, I looked at Courtney and asked, "Girl, what do you want right now?"

She laughed. "To get the hell of out of here."

"I don't think that's what you *really* want. Let's be real. What do you want, sister?"

"No, really," Courtney said. "I just want to get out of this store." A tear formed in the corner of her eye as she looked away.

"I know, Court," I said, pushing my luck, "but I don't think that's what you really want. Dig deep, girl, and tell me what you *actually* want right now."

"I just want to feel *good* again, even beautiful! I want to stop looking in the mirror and hating what I see. I want to stop feeling so angry and disappointed with myself."

We both heard it at the same time. We were at the root of her fear, and it extended far beyond the size of her clothes, a label that defines so many of us. She was disappointed, an emotion too many of us are far too familiar with. As painful as it was for her to admit, this was the first step to her being able to reclaim both her beauty and her confidence; she had to acknowledge the type of change she wanted to make. She wanted to feel better. It wasn't about clothes but her emotional well-being.

Almost as quickly as she confessed that out loud, I felt her energy shift a little bit. I squeezed her arm. A flicker of hope flashed on her face as we made it to the plus-sized floor and were greeted with beautiful displays of gorgeous clothing. Just like the other floors, we were surrounded by many options: they had business, they had casual, they had party, and they had fancy. We both saw the high-end clothing at the same time. Courtney had never envisioned herself in stunning high-end clothing before.

By acknowledging and then articulating the change she wanted to see in her life, she was already making room for that change, and she saw her reality a bit differently.

Armed with a sense of purpose, we looked for clothes designed for her body now, not how it used to be or how she hoped it would be again. We looked for outfits that would accentuate and showcase her beauty and the person she was today.

I knew her closet was full of clothes she hung on to from before having kids. She was holding on to a version of herself she had outgrown. She wasn't ready to get rid of them, even though it had been five years since her last child was born.

We agreed that I would serve as her personal shopper and that she would try on everything I brought to the change room, even if her initial reaction wasn't favorable. It wasn't hard. The store had so many amazing pieces that I thought would look incredible on her: sexy tops, powerful suits, playful dresses, and everything in between. Soon her change room was overflowing!

When the sales associate came by to check on us, she seemed a bit concerned by the fact that we had well over twenty items in a fitting room and a pile outside propped up against a sign that read "Three items maximum, please!"

But all it took was a little wink and a gentle smile to get the sales associate on board. I whispered, "We are having a transformation over here." She smiled back, obviously eager to help, and ignored our clothing limit infraction.

First Courtney tried on a pair of jeans. "Oh my God, I *love* these! I haven't worn jeans even *once* since having my kiddos. I live in leggings."

We were only getting started, and she was already warming up to the possibility that she didn't have to wait until she lost weight to feel good about herself again and look good too. Of course, not every outfit looked great. Some were "too red," some fit too big or too small, and some were "old-lady clothes." But there were quite a few options that brought out her best features, as clothes are supposed to, and I noticed her looking at herself in the mirror with a growing appreciation.

With a pile of keepers set aside, she tried on the final piece and looked herself over slowly from top to bottom. On the rack, it had been a cute red dress, but when she put it on, it became a smokin' hot red dress. It couldn't have looked better; it seemed custom made for her.

I stood beside her and gently put my hand on her shoulder. "*Look* at yourself, sister! Really look, okay? Can you see the gorgeous woman that I'm seeing right now?"

She replied with a smile.

Seizing the moment, I said, "Repeat after me. 'I. Am. Beautiful!'"

After a long pause, she whispered, "I am beautiful."

"Again, but tell your eyes this time. Look at yourself."

She narrowed in on her gaze in the mirror, catching a sneak peek into her future. She then said, "I am beautiful."

"Let's do it one more time, but together, okay?"

We looked at ourselves in the mirror and proclaimed, "I. Am. Beautiful!"

Courtney's body shivered gently, as if releasing something that it no longer needed, her spine straightening and her shoulders pulling back in response. She was covered in goosebumps. She looked three inches taller than she had an hour ago.

She came out wearing some jeans and a gorgeous blue top. She grabbed her old clothes and tossed them in the garbage bin at the cashier counter. "I won't be needing those anymore," she said with a twinkle in her eye. We paid for all her new outfits and left, and it was clear that she was leaving more than her old clothes behind. She was leaving behind an old version of herself who had been waiting to feel worthy before making a change.

"I am going to donate my old clothes when I get back home and make room in my closet for the new me who is coming out."

I smiled from ear to ear and fist-pumped the air.

"That's what I'm talking about," I said. "Sometimes you have to let go to make space for something that fits you better."

Change Can Start Small

Making change is hard, and acknowledging the type of change you want to make can be the hardest part. In Courtney's case, the change seems small—buying clothes that fit and flatter her—but the real change was that she wanted to allow herself to feel beautiful again, to see her own worth, and to no longer feel disappointed with herself. More often than not, the change that we're making is window dressing for the change we really want. She was stuck on the physical change, but the emotional change was more significant. Losing weight might be part of the process for some of us, but if we identify what's underneath the desire to lose weight, we can make change that is more important and longer lasting.

Because she hadn't yet recognized the *internal* change she wanted to make—it wasn't something she had considered before—she had been unable to make the external physical one. Once she became aware that what she *really* wanted was to feel beautiful and worthy again, she was able to take the next step. In our case, that was a step up to the floor that was right for her.

We left Macy's that day with a few bags of clothes, smiling and proud. We had gone to find some great deals, and we had left with more than we could have imagined. Courtney found her confidence again and claimed a new version of herself, one that continued to serve her for many years after. Her energy seemed lighter in an instant. Once again, I saw what is possible when we stop waiting for permission to change and decide to give that permission to ourselves.

Our little shopping trip started a transformation in Courtney's identity. A year later, she was invited to accept a prestigious business leadership award. In the past, she would have dressed all in black with a cardigan sweater draped on top to blend in. But not this new version of Courtney. Nope. She busted out that red dress from Macy's to accept her award and owned it onstage. I'd never see her that confident before, and I was so proud of the transformation that she had brought into her life. I clapped so hard, my hands hurt, and my eyes were filled with tears, knowing what this award meant for her. She

**Sometimes you
have to let go
to make space**
for something that
fits you better.

received external validation that she was more than worthy and didn't need to wait any longer. She was a wise businesswoman taking center stage of her own life.

What started as a small change—wearing clothes that fit her and made her feel good—became a major life transformation. When she decided to lead her own life, she stepped into a new leadership style in business, which was recognized by others. With her newfound confidence, she had more energy, her business boomed, and her relationships improved. That's the nature of confidence. It doesn't usually stay contained to one area of our life; it transfers over into other areas without any additional effort.

Now she's just fine wearing plus-sized clothes; it doesn't cause her to shrink back and hide anymore. Forcing herself into outfits that no longer fit was not serving her or anyone else. She also stopped trying to squeeze herself into relationships or environments that no longer fit her. While she accepted the plus-sized label, she never again let that label define her worth. For the first time in years, she defined her worthiness not by the number on the scale or the tag on her clothes but by the appreciation she had for herself. Her view of herself changed, and so other people's views of her changed too. People commented on how great she looked and asked her if she'd lost weight. She would often reply, "I didn't lose weight, but I gained self-acceptance." She is proud of her journey and encourages others to discover their journey and commit to the change they want before they feel ready.

When Courtney rode up that escalator to the next floor, she upleveled her life in the process. When we change our mindset to acknowledge that positive change is possible, even when it's uncomfortable, we make room for significant changes to unfold in our lives.

When we choose to embrace the next version of ourselves—whether it's about finding a community that supports us, a job that energizes us, or relationships that fuel us—we have to adjust our relationship with change. We need to see change with a new lens. Change is a good thing. Change is positive. We are meant to experience changes in our life and change within ourselves. In order to feel better about ourselves, we need to get clear on what we *really* want, the change we want to make, and give ourselves permission to step out and to step up.

Take a moment to reflect on your life using the following questions as prompts. What change do you want to make in your life? What is standing in the way of you revealing the next version of yourself? Where are you hiding or trying to squeeze yourself into a mold that no longer fits you? What labels are you attached to, or trying to avoid, that are causing you more stress than necessary? What floor of life is no longer where you belong, and how can you rise up? Where do you want to go, and who do you want to become? What type of change do you want to make, and is there a feeling underneath that you can identify?

Feelings Move Us into Action

As with Courtney, learning to identify the change you want in your life starts on a deeper level—with your feelings. So many of us jump into action and do the thing we think we need to do to get the results we think we need to make. If we don't deeply connect with what is driving the desire for change, we will not stay committed to the change for the long term. For the best kinds of changes, first understand the relationship of your mind, body, and soul to change and how it can align with who you are and how it will serve you in the process.

In our culture, feelings often get a bad rap. We're taught to treat them with suspicion and to ignore them as much as possible. If they are one of the "bad" emotions, like anger, sadness, anxiety, or fear, we desperately try to suppress them.

But to ignore them is to bypass so much of what it means to be human. Feelings provide valuable information that help us navigate and support the change we want to make. They connect us to others, connect us with our bodies, and connect us with the environment around us. They are constantly providing us with relevant information at the speed of instinct, acting as our body's internal navigation system. Ignoring them makes us less aware and less able to make decisions that will best serve us and our future. If we ignore our feelings and our intuition, we stifle our emotional intelligence too.

Baba Shiv, professor of marketing at Stanford Graduate School of Business, notes that research shows that roughly 95 percent of all our decisions are "shaped by emotion," with the remainder from a logical state. Although that percentage is an estimate, there is a wide and growing body of neurological research to support the general thesis. We make decisions based on our feelings, so feelings are, in fact, important.

When we tune into our feelings, we aren't actually *changing* anything; that part gets to be a choice. We're gathering information about the quiet forces that drive our behavior; we're making the subconscious conscious. Moving forward with less awareness means we're moving forward with less information.

Our feelings also provide contour for our lives. Our feelings give individual moments meaning, each one contributing to a beautiful mosaic, if we have the eyes to see it. Without emotions, there would be no art, no dance, no music, no love, no desire, no passion, and no meaning to our existence.

Courtney's transformation began when she allowed herself to feel, and then express, the shame and disappointment she felt for not meeting the standard for how she thought she should look. Before she was able to fully identify, articulate, and feel her emotions, she hid behind her baggy clothes and played small in her life. By acknowledging her deepest emotions, she was able to use them as information and make a new decision. That decision ultimately had a ripple effect on her entire life. BFCs always have the opportunity to make a profound impact on you, often changing the trajectory of your life.

For those of us who are mothers, going from womanhood into motherhood changes every aspect of ourselves. Our physical, mental, emotional, relational, and social changes are massive. Why on earth would we expect ourselves to be the people we were before having babies? Yet we put pressure on ourselves to be physically, mentally, and emotionally the same.

If you are doubting that the big change you want to make is possible for you, it's helpful to think back on moments in your life before now when you made a big change. How did you feel beforehand? What motivated you to make that change? Once you let that sink in, you can access those same emotions to propel you forward into future change. Once you understand the skill of making changes, you can make change in many different areas of your life using the same road map. My Get Unstuck, Cycle of Change Model will help you make the BFCs you want.

If you're having trouble accessing those emotions, here are a few questions that I find helpful. I believe that at the root of our intentions, we are motivated primarily by two emotions: fear and love. We move away from something to avoid the fear (avoiding pain), or we move toward something to feel love (experience pleasure). So, take a moment to reflect on these three questions and see what comes up for you. Pay attention to what you want in your life that makes you feel good, or what you are avoiding because of the discomfort.

1. **What Am I Moving Away From?** What discomfort are you moving away from that is no longer aligned with who you are or is no longer serving you? Pay attention to your frustrations and the friction in your life to identify what you are moving away from. For example, perhaps you are moving away from having toxic people (fear and pain) in your life, and you don't like how you feel after you interact with them.

2. **What Am I Moving Toward?** What is the desired outcome you want to achieve? Think about the feelings, experiences, and realities you want. For example, you want relationships that lift you up, and you are moving toward creating better boundaries, so that you feel better about yourself (love) and enjoy positive relationships (pleasure).

3. **What Do I Want to Feel Instead?** What is the feeling you wish to experience from the change you have been contemplating? It's not enough to focus on the change itself but the *feeling* attached to that change. By putting boundaries in place and taking care of your needs, you are making relationship changes, and you want to feel comfortable (love) and encouraged rather than discouraged and uncomfortable (fear). By focusing on experiencing more positive

emotions and feeling comfortable, you can focus on experiencing this change.

When I'm in my role as a business coach, my clients often come to me with specific problems in their businesses that they'd like us to address together. They come with a problem and hope to leave with a solution. As in any other area, they are moving away from fear/pain and toward love/reward. Fair enough. But if we only focus on the *outcome* itself, we miss many important steps along the way that keep us accountable and in motion. When we focus on the feelings, we get down to the root of the problem and find a sustainable solution for the long term. Focusing on feelings rather than outcomes provides us with more fulfillment in our lives and greater chances for success. Feelings move us forward.

The Backstory Behind the Feeling

On group coaching calls working with the Dance Studio Owners Association, more than 90 percent of the questions that come in stem from a lack of confidence in some area, though the owners do not realize it. None of us do. Fear shows up in many different hats: not feeling ready, not feeling good enough, not having enough time, not having enough energy, or not believing change is possible. Entrepreneurs are problem solvers, but sometimes we dance around hard conversations, push aside conflict, and avoid making decisions because it's easier in the moment. We all feel uncomfortable having hard conversations, so we often avoid them, though they are necessary to have. Sometimes the most important conversations we can have are with ourselves.

Before the members ask their questions, they usually start by sharing a backstory that led them to their current conflict. The backstory provides information, details, and, in a way, a justification to explain why they are in this current situation. Time and time again, I sense that there is a feeling each one of them has buried deep down related to fear and worthiness. We all lack something, and whatever our something is, it usually shows up in our backstory. It's often not the situation itself but the story we have told ourselves to give it meaning that we need to look at to gain clarity.

On one group call, Sally shared her own backstory before she asked her question. "I feel so unappreciated. I work fourteen hours per day, and I feel as though my employees don't appreciate me. I'm exhausted. I'm so busy, and I'm not making any money. I feel like giving up."

I listened to her and validated Sally's feelings because they are real. Then I asked, "How do you *want* to feel instead of being exhausted and unappreciated?"

After a long pause, she answered, "I want to have fun and feel alive again."

Like most high-achieving people, Sally placed having fun as a last priority on her list. Most of the time, it wasn't even *on* the list. I understand and experience this pressure myself as an entrepreneur. We feel obligated to keep completing tasks because we carry a great sense of responsibility and care for our team, customers, and services.

We tend to measure our days by how productive we were, rather than how good we felt. We tell ourselves that once everything is done, we will have time for fun. Once we finally have some time, we don't want to do anything because we feel exhausted. I've been there many times, and like Sally, I need to pay attention when I fall into this trap. Being in the business of busyness is not good for anyone.

Sometimes we get so caught up in *doing* that we forget to take time for *being*. It can seem easier to *push* through, rather than *pause* to feel the feelings. By acknowledging how she felt, Sally was able to uncover what she truly wanted. Feeling unappreciated by her team was symptomatic. She hadn't been appreciating *herself* for years, and her team amplified this feeling for her. With this change in perspective, Sally gave herself permission to let loose and have some fun. She took baby steps and made the changes she needed to free up pockets of time and put better boundaries in place. She started taking more opportunities to care for herself and learn to appreciate herself, not just for what she could do in a day but for who she was. This was the

You are the one common factor in your entire life, including your experiences and your potential.

change she needed to make. She needed to make an *emotional* change so that things could shift in her business and personal life.

Soon, the spark in her eyes returned. She got her groove back because she found appreciation for herself and discovered her backstory—what was really preventing her from making change in her business and personal life. Sally never felt appreciated by her partner, had an ex who had been verbally abusive, and accepted this as her normal baseline, without understanding where her backstory came from and how it continued to show up in her personal and professional life. She always jumped in to save people, jumped in to put out fires. With all of the jumping in, she had nothing left for herself. She felt a sense of worthiness from jumping in, helping people, and solving issues, but in reality she needed to help herself. This is so common with people pleasers who have "the disease to please." We do it automatically without even noticing what we are doing, and we fail to understand that we have a limited amount of energy and need to take care of ourselves too.

When Sally wasn't pouring from an empty cup, she became a better leader, and her relationships at home improved too. Her emotional change also triggered intellectual, social, and vocational changes.

No matter what your circumstance is or what change you want to make, when you focus on your emotional state first, you will gain clarity.

The Makeup of Change

We can make many different changes in life. We can think of different categories of change by using the eight components of wellness. According to the University of Maryland, wellness has eight mutually interdependent aspects: vocational, social, physical, intellectual, financial, environmental, emotional, and spiritual. As researcher Debbie L. Stoewen writes, "Attention must be given to all the dimensions, as neglect of any one over time will adversely affect the others, and ultimately one's health, well-being, and quality of life."

Isn't that what we all crave? A high-quality life and to feel well? Looking at ourselves with these eight dimensions in mind, ask yourself what part of you is feeling disconnected, overwhelmed, or discouraged. These eight dimensions of the human experience make us whole, and they are also the parts of us that experience change. In my confidence coaching sessions, we tackle one area first and then work on the others, since everything is connected. Take a moment to reflect on the type of change you wish to make the most and use the dimension of wellness to identify the types of change needed.

1. **Vocational Change: What You Do for Work** Maybe you love your line of work but are ready for new challenges and a higher income. You'd like a promotion but don't feel ready to put yourself up for it. Maybe you're not that into your line of work anymore or, worse, never have been. You feel like your talent and potential are being wasted, and you want to move into a different career altogether. Or you're tired of working to make other people money and want to be your own boss. You see the freedom that other entrepreneurs have to make their own schedules, without a salary cap, and you want that freedom for yourself.

2. **Social Change: Your Relationships with Others** Let's face it: people change over time, and sometimes relationships that were once a great fit no longer are. This happens for a number of reasons, many of which are no one's fault. I have met a number of women over the years who were, in my opinion, long overdue for a relationship overhaul, who were stuck in marriages in which they were undervalued and unappreciated. Other times, the relationships that need change are with a particular friend or friend group. You realize that those relationships are dragging you down, but you don't know how to end or adjust them well.

3. **Physical Change: Your Body and Appearance** The relationship you have with your own body is the most important relationship each of us will ever have. It's through our body that we experience everything that life has to offer and it's how we offer our best to the

world around us. Yet so often we don't recognize the importance of taking care of our bodies until we get a wake-up call. That wake-up call can be a glance in the mirror, or it can be a medical diagnosis or even a lack of energy. Whatever the catalyst, you want to change the way you look, how you move, how you feel, the habits you have, or even how you feel in your own skin.

4. **Intellectual Change: Mindset and Learning** You're looking to step into a new level of understanding. This change is often made by going to school to learn something new, but not always. It may be a new challenging task that requires more mental capacity. It may be challenging yourself to think differently about a task you are facing to get different results. Anything that stretches your mindset is an intellectual change.

5. **Financial Change: Your Relationship to Money** Maybe you're looking to make a change in your relationship with money. Maybe you want to spend less, make more, or look at finances differently. Or maybe your finances have shifted dramatically for better or worse, and you need to change how you manage your money. Your viewpoint on money impacts your decisions and the actions you take.

6. **Environmental Change: The Places That Surround You** You may want to move to a new neighborhood, a new state, a new country, or a new house that you feel would suit you better. It can be as grand as moving to a new place or as simple as clearing your space and redecorating your home or workplace. You feel like a change in your physical environment would give you a better life.

7. **Emotional Change: How You Feel About Yourself and Your Life** If your relationship with yourself or others is not where you'd like it to be, you recognize the need for some growth in this area. Paying attention to your emotional state in relation to others and to your reality can initiate change. Asking yourself how you want to feel is a great way to spark emotional change. Being able to regulate your emotions in response to others is the ultimate emotional change we want to strive for.

8. **Spiritual Change: Your Connection to Something Greater Than Yourself** Maybe it's time for you to lose your religion... or find it. As you grow, your relationship with the great mysteries of life changes. Perhaps you feel stuck in your current community or with old beliefs that don't serve you any longer. Or maybe you feel a longing in your soul to connect with your spiritual side. The desire to connect to something greater than yourself is a spiritual change whether it's to a set religion or a pathway with the universe or energetic fields. It's an energy and belief that extends beyond your life.

Considering these eight dimensions of wellness will help us identify where change needs to be made first. Remember, you can change in many areas, but a BFC is composed of a set of smaller steps that are put into motion through preparation. By embracing and focusing on one main area of change, you avoid getting stuck in the procrastination and perfection loop, unsure of what to do and waiting for the perfect time.

Courtney first had to make an *intellectual* change that it was safe for her to buy new clothes, which happened after she acknowledged the *emotional* change she wanted to make. She had to identify that her *physical* body had changed, before she could move to the correct floor. Changing her mindset about what was possible for her now, and understanding how she really felt, changed her *emotional* state and allowed her to show up in the world with more confidence. She connected back to herself in a *spiritual* way, seeing herself again after she'd abandoned herself for years; she started trusting that the universe had her back. She started to trust people and life again because she trusted herself, which made her change *socially* too. Once she changed her relationship with herself, all her relationships changed, including her *vocational* satisfaction. This improved her bottom line and created *financial* change. She started taking holidays again, traveling and experiencing *environmental* changes. She put herself out there more, unafraid to be seen. She started trusting herself again, and things changed for her.

Going up the escalator and taking that first step allowed her to step into her greatness in all aspects of her life. What floor do you need to give yourself permission to visit?

It's time to give yourself permission to change and know that you can do this. You are valuable, you are worthy, and you will be okay. Here is your cue, the sign you have been waiting for, and your gentle, loving nudge. You are the one common factor in your entire life, including your experiences and your potential. No one else—only you! It's your responsibility to make your life great and start the process before you feel ready.

 Hand on Heart

Take a moment to affirm yourself by saying this aloud:

It's okay to make change, and I am qualified to claim the change I want in my life.

Take a moment to reflect on the type of change you are experiencing, and try to identify it as something outside yourself rather than part of your identity.

I am experiencing this _____ type of change and am open to changing.

Lie down, close your eyes, and focus on your breathing. Take nice full breaths in through your nose and out through your mouth. Let your tongue melt from the roof of your mouth to the bottom. Place your hand on your heart, and ask yourself these questions:

> *What is the change I want to make?*
> *Why is this change important?*
> *How do I want to feel when I make this change?*
>
> Whatever comes to your mind first, pay attention, say it out loud, and ask yourself the question *"Why do I want that?"*
>
> Keep asking yourself the question *why* to discover your real motivation and to tap into your feelings. You may do this several times until you reach a real moment of clarity. Once you get to the why, ask yourself how. How will you go about making this change?

P.S. Claim the change you want to make.
Step out to step up.

4
UPDATE YOUR MINDSET

"The greatest discovery of all time is that a person can change [their] future by merely changing [their] attitude."

OPRAH WINFREY

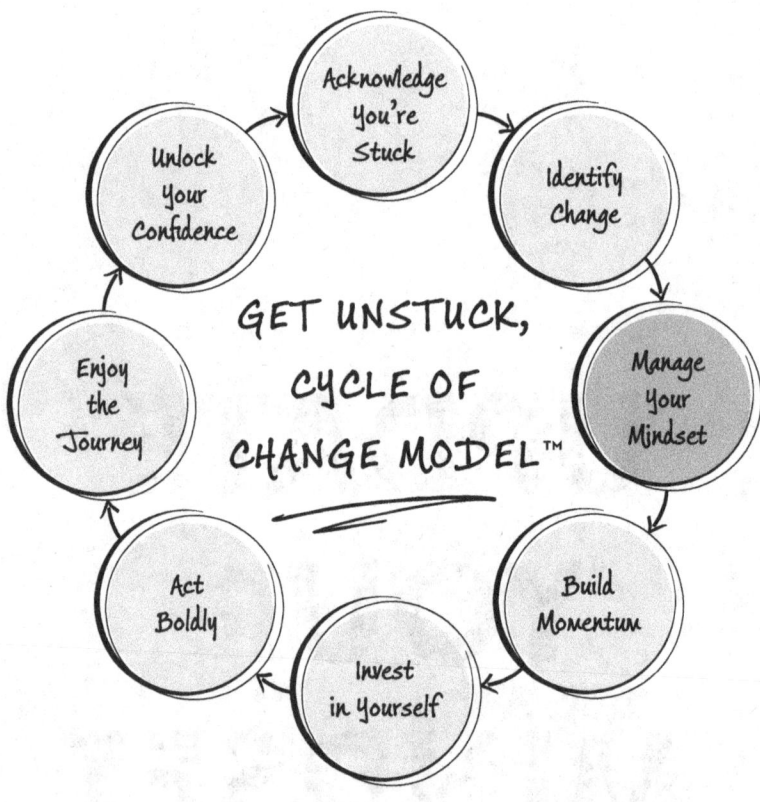

The mind is where the magic happens. After you have acknowledged you are stuck and you identify the change you need, it's time to focus on updating and managing your mindset. When your mind is positive and strong, you are more likely to take the necessary steps forward.

IN 2018, I ATTENDED a conference in New York City to help me upgrade my marketing skills. Whenever possible, after an intense time of growth or learning, I like to take time to decompress and process what I've learned before rushing home. Taking this time is even better when I can do it with a friend, and I was lucky that one of my closest friends, my other friend from Power of Three, was attending the same conference. Amanda and I sat together in my hotel room in cozy pajamas and talked for hours. We talked about the challenges of being entrepreneurs, the opportunities, the excitement, and the heavy workloads we carried as mothers and business owners. In a conversation about a new marketing idea I had for my dance studio, Amanda stopped me mid-sentence and said, "Wow, Cara, you're *soooo* brilliant."

My body reacted faster than I could process what she said, my head jerking backward as my eyes filled with tears. It was an unexpected reaction to a compliment from my dear friend. The combination of her words and her sincerity caught me off guard. I knew that I wasn't *un*intelligent, but nobody had ever called me brilliant before.

Growing up, I was lucky to have wonderful parents who loved me well and affirmed me often, and my teachers always encouraged me too. But I had never seen myself in that light. In fact, I viewed myself as very much the opposite. I thought that if you were brilliant, things would come easy for you, and that has never been true for me. I always had to work hard for results.

As the emotions caught me by surprise, I started explaining my reaction to Amanda. I said through tears, "I had to work really hard for good grades in school from elementary to university. I really struggled with reading and writing in elementary and was always a few years behind my classmates. So, I worked extremely hard, sought extra help from my teachers, attended a learning center after school, and... still always came in at the bottom of my class while attending elementary and junior high school."

I realized then that after all these years, I was still carrying with me a remnant of the shame I had felt as a young child. That shame was clinging to the edges of my heart. Here I was, a grown-ass woman, graduated with two degrees with top grades, running two successful businesses, coaching thousands of entrepreneurs, speaking internationally, and I was still operating under the limiting belief that I really wasn't all that smart. That limiting belief still played a role in how I viewed myself and shaped my mindset without me even realizing it.

"The insecurity I felt in elementary school, from comparing myself to my classmates, grew in high school. My judgment was clouded, and I doubted my ability to get into university," I realized aloud. "I assumed I got over that when I graduated with top grades, but I think it's still there a little bit. I work hard to get results in everything I do and have never viewed myself as brilliant but as a hard worker."

This may be true for you too: my early childhood experiences were a breeding ground for limiting beliefs that I still carried without awareness. After I reflected on my emotional state, I had to explore where else these insecurities showed up so I could release them and update my mindset. "What else is holding me back?" I wondered.

Amanda never knew me as a child and was shocked to learn that I had struggled with a learning disability. She saw me through a different lens as the woman I was now, not the girl I used to be. "Sister, I've *never* seen you as anything other than brilliant! Look at what you've accomplished. You are a brilliant badass businesswoman! You need to own that!"

What if, just for a moment, I let that feeling in? What if I allowed myself to believe that I was not inferior to others but could stand out in a crowd? Maybe the learning disability didn't define me as much as my ability to overcome it did. Maybe the years I had spent hustling to grow myself personally and intellectually actually meant something. Maybe... just maybe, I *was* brilliant.

The pain even **contributed to my gain.**

Amanda's sincere encouragement presented me with an opportunity to *replace* one belief with another: "I'm not that smart, but I work hard" with "I work hard, and maybe... I'm also brilliant." It was time for me to update my mindset and let go of what wasn't serving me.

The next morning, as I was applying my makeup, and still feeling the glow of my time with Amanda, I remembered my trip with Courtney to Macy's. I had invited Courtney to say "I am beautiful" over and over while looking in the mirror. I offered myself a similar invitation to tap into the intellectual change I desired. Looking in the mirror, I said, "I. Am. Brilliant."

Although I wasn't sure that I fully believed it yet, it did seem to land in my heart with more weight than I expected. Repeating it a few more times, my resistance lessened, and my acceptance increased. I also noticed how clear and vibrant my eyes were. I hadn't ever really noticed the colors before: the way the dark brown in the center dripping like paint onto the sides in a streaked transition into green. As I noticed that new little beauty of my eyes, I also felt a warmth spread through my body, as if honey was coating my insides. It was a mixture of love for myself, gratitude for my friend, and compassion for the younger version of me who had carried the weight of that limiting belief all those years. I was different now, and it was okay to let that version of myself go.

The disappointment, frustration, and embarrassment that had played quite a role in my life for decades were being replaced with admiration and love. The pain even contributed to my gain. Without the challenges, I wouldn't have developed my strong work ethic and mental determination. Perhaps I could accept that I was in fact brilliant.

Years have passed, and I still choose to carry this new belief with me. Every time I start to feel even just a little unintelligent, I pause and offer up the alternative. "Well, maybe that's true," I say to myself with compassion. "Or maybe... I'm brilliant!" Each time I believe it just a little bit more, and that new belief has become my default.

When we notice old beliefs come up that are not serving us anymore, we are presented with a choice: to reinforce them or to upgrade our mindset. Most of the time, we reinforce these old beliefs without even noticing that we're doing it. That's why they've become so well established. We've literally practiced those thoughts thousands of times in our lives.

Dr. Fred Luskin of Stanford University says that the average person has roughly sixty thousand thoughts every single day. That's about 1.5 thoughts every single second. Of those thoughts, 90 percent are believed to be recurring and repetitive thoughts. What I love about this is that when we are intentional about changing a belief and we put in the effort to keep our new belief top of mind, after a while our brains will start to do much of the heavy lifting for us. We retread those new thoughts over and over and over again each day.

Without realizing it, Amanda had tripped one of my old beliefs and, in the same breath, gave me an invitation to replace it with a new one. People who love and know us well frequently help us to upgrade our mindset. They often have a more realistic and holistic view of us, and their perspectives can help lead the way into new beliefs that serve us better. Our tendency might be to brush off compliments. Next time you receive a compliment, I encourage you to let it sink in for a moment and say thank you. If your internal voice reacts strongly, as in my case, there may be an invitation there for you to update your mindset.

What Is Holding You Back?

I don't want to discount your own personal experience. I understand how hard it can be to replace old beliefs with new ones, *especially* those that were formed in childhood, and even more so for those formed in hardship or trauma. Every one of us is shaped by entirely different circumstances. We didn't all have supportive parents or teachers. We may not have been truly valued or affirmed and may have felt the need to search for validation elsewhere. Some of us experienced trauma that robbed us of the foundation we so clearly deserved. I have some dear friends who fall into those categories, and I can't even imagine what that was like for them. And yet, as one of them said to me recently, "Sometimes, the further you have to go, the more you get to enjoy the journey." I've noticed that my friends who have experienced the deepest childhood wounds are most focused on upgrading their mindsets. They had to in order to survive abuse, trauma, or the early death of a parent. They recognize that the path forward is always in the direction of a new mindset, and they don't want to remain stuck in the negative beliefs that were handed down to them.

Regardless of whether your path up to now has been relatively easy or an obstacle course over landmines, we have all adopted beliefs that may have served us for a time but no longer do. We can usually tell which beliefs serve us the least by the internal reaction we have to them. Do they elevate us, or do they make us feel small? Do they give us a sense of hope for the future, or do they fill us with fear? Do they give us a reason to love ourselves more or less?

If they tear us down, they are beliefs worth changing. If they build us up, they are beliefs worth reinforcing. It's that simple.

Now, you might be thinking, "Cara, I hear what you're saying, but I don't want to be *delusional*. Not every positive thing I think is true about me. I really *am* bad with money. I'm not brave, not successful, not creative, not good at relationships, and not even capable of becoming any of those things. I get what you're saying, but I'm not so sure."

The things you believe about yourself in part create the reality that you live out every single day. Maybe you have far more control over the direction your life takes than you think. Maybe you don't see yourself and your inherent God-given beauty accurately. Maybe you believe you're "bad with money" and are living into that belief. Maybe you're courageous and capable of immense levels of success. Maybe you have secret access to an abundant well of intuition and creativity. You have a deep knowledge of how to love and be loved, which is the central skill required to build beautiful relationships, and it's coded in your very DNA. We are all born for connection. If all of that's true—which I believe it is—then maybe, just maybe, you, my dear, are also brilliant. There is brilliance in you waiting to come out. You don't need to wait any longer to tap into it. By becoming more of yourself, you step into your brilliance.

The question is not *if* you're any of those things, but *how* you can release them from within you and express them to their fullest extent. Every time we believe in and allow limiting beliefs to hold us back, we dim our brilliance. But they don't have to be true. We get to decide. *You* get to decide.

What beliefs are keeping you small and holding you back right now? To step into a Big Freakin' Change, we're going to need every advantage we can get. So, take some time to consider what limiting beliefs you may be holding on to and what you might like to replace them with.

Most often, we can tap into our limiting beliefs through our emotions. When strong emotions aren't coming up for us in the moment, we can look at other indicators that an upgrade to our mindset would be beneficial. What repeating themes and patterns show up in your life that you wish wouldn't? What is something you wish you could change about yourself, or something you want to stop tolerating? Where are you feeling stressed? Do you consistently have relationships that end in conflict? Or do you tend to run late for everything? Wherever we see a pattern in our life that we'd like to change, there is a belief behind it that can be swapped out for something more useful.

Go ahead and try this exercise:

- What are three limiting beliefs that regularly play in your mind?
- What are possible alternatives to those beliefs?
- Repeat the positive alternatives. Then give yourself permission to update your mindset.

Just like with our emotions, the information that we get by asking ourselves questions, we can evaluate and then use to move forward.

How Our Mindset Holds Us Back

Imagine you want to change jobs and leave a toxic work environment because of the social relationships. Even though you know it's not healthy, you waffle on the decision daily because there is a part of you that is scared to make a vocational change. As painful as it is, this workplace has served you in some way, and you don't want to add more stress to your plate.

Maybe you don't want to show yourself fully to the world, or you play small in life because your default belief is that this is "just life" and wanting more is selfish or unreasonable. As a result, you end up justifying and tolerating your toxic workplace. You convince yourself it's not *that bad* and you can learn to manage the drama, while desperately clinging to any positives. You compare your reality to other people's job satisfaction and try to hang on to hope. But it keeps you up at night, and you get stuck in overthinking and feeling frustrated with yourself.

Perhaps the career change you're contemplating is into an entirely different industry and position. You know you've outgrown your current job and want to apply for a management position in a new sector. You update your résumé and read the job post several times, ensuring you check all the boxes. Insecurities rush in, and you talk yourself out of even applying. You think, "What's the point? There is probably someone better for the position." You remind yourself how old you are, assuming they want someone younger than you because they learn more quickly. You tell yourself they want someone older than you with more experience. Regardless, you believe you don't measure up. You decide to make the best out of your current position, convincing yourself that it's good enough and you shouldn't complain.

In both examples of job change, your perception of the situation and of yourself creates your reality. What you believe in your mind transpires. The possibility of making change starts with working on your beliefs about yourself and choosing to think differently. As Dr. Wayne Dyer famously said, "Change your thoughts. Change your life."

Your mind is where the magic is. Focus on the thoughts that run through your mind and see where you could benefit from an update. Start with one area at a time, and notice the subtle differences in how you think and how you feel. Your thoughts, feelings, and actions are all connected.

Take a moment to reflect on the areas of your life that you find yourself justifying or tolerating, where you may catch yourself saying, "I'm just not ready." You wrestle back and forth between what your heart yearns for and what limiting beliefs tell you is possible. Our heart sees potential and wants more, but our head wants to keep us safe with consistency and avoid loss, even when it's not serving us.

It's critical to remind ourselves that change is hard and that our brains are wired for safety and not success. As I shared in chapter 1, our brains are wired to resist change and will often give us a million reasons to stick with the status quo. If your brain is telling you that you're not ready, know it's doing its job to try to keep you safe! Override this alert and take action anyway.

In my experience, we get to lead more satisfying lives when we focus our attention on the possibilities set before us rather than the problems that consume us. We do that by adopting a growth mindset, believing we are made for more and can evolve.

The term "growth mindset" was coined by world-renowned Stanford University psychologist Carol Dweck. She suggests that there are two types of mindsets: growth and fixed. With a growth mindset, we believe that abilities can be developed over time and that we can evolve and further develop our potential. With a fixed mindset, we believe that abilities are set and predetermined. Adopting a growth mindset means choosing possibilities and working toward them, believing we can always improve. Here are some simple examples of a growth mindset:

"I may be a beginner with spreadsheets, but I can learn the basics from YouTube."

"Sure, I'm new to working out, but I can attend a class and learn the basics."

"I am new to cooking, but I will read some recipe books to learn some cooking techniques."

A growth mindset leads us to identify the possibilities and solutions in our life: to make a plan, develop new skills, and trust that we are capable. One of my favorite entrepreneurs, Marie Forleo, epitomizes this every time she says, "Everything is figureoutable." If we adopt this mindset that everything is "figureoutable," and that you are brilliant, imagine the endless possibilities you can tap into.

In contrast, a fixed mindset caps your potential based on where you already are. It assumes that our skill sets and character qualities are immutable and predetermined, and the best we can hope for is more of the same, unless Lady Luck pays a visit.

Here are some examples of a fixed mindset:

"I'm not good with numbers and can't do spreadsheets, even though I wish I had that gift."

"I wish I could get fitter. Some people are just lucky like that, but not me, unfortunately."

"I suck at cooking. My friends make great meals when they have me over for dinner. But I order in when I have them over."

A fixed mindset identifies problems, assumes nothing can be changed, and sees potential as predetermined, often defending one's behavior as "this is just the way I am." We can and should strive to fill our lives with a sense of possibility, and a growth mindset helps us to get there. We are meant to grow and evolve. The reality is we often have a mix of growth mindset in one area and fixed mindset in another.

When you decide to update how you view yourself and consider new possibilities, you are choosing to adopt a growth mindset. This is how you grow as a person, in your profession, in your relationships with others, and in your life. A growth mindset supports you making a BFC. Adopting a growth mindset can be as simple as repeating, "I will be open to growth and have a growth mindset," "I am brilliant," or "I believe in positive possibilities." Look for opportunities within your problems, and be curious about what else is possible.

Making "updates to your system" may not agree with your brain at first, but that's not a reason to avoid change. Change is uncomfortable and necessary if you want to uplevel your life. Let's discover how to make a BFC. It's easier than you think.

Reflect, Release, Replace

Now that we're looking at our lives through the lens of growth and possibility, it's time to actually update our mindset. I'm going to share with you the process that I personally follow and that I use with my dance students, coaching clients, and my family and friends.

There are three simple steps to this process, each one building on the one before. The steps are reflect, release, and replace.

First, we start by *reflecting* on our lives through the lens of our emotions and our patterns to identify where a change in our beliefs would most serve us. Second, we make a conscious choice to *release* those old emotions and patterns with love. Finally, we identify what we'd like to *replace* those old beliefs with, connecting them to the positive emotions we'd like to feel.

If you already know what your Big Freakin' Change is, then walk through these steps with that in mind. If you have yet to identify your Big Freakin' Change, then walk through these steps in relation to your life in general.

1. **Reflect:** Look at your life as it is presently and at patterns from the past to identify areas where a mindset change would be useful. Ask yourself what could be better.

   Start with the Heart: What challenging emotions am I experiencing, or have I experienced in the past, that I'd like to change? Where am I feeling dissatisfied, overwhelmed, disconnected, unfulfilled, or unaligned in my life?

   Identify Your Patterns: What negative patterns seem to show up in my life that I'd like to end?

   Identify the Belief: What do these emotions and patterns say about me, my ability to change, and my future potential?

2. **Release:** How do I let go of these old beliefs to make room for new ones?

Feel It to Change It: Look at the beliefs you'd like to change, and connect to the specific emotions you feel about them. Allow yourself to feel your emotions as fully as possible in the moment, without being overwhelmed by them.

Release with Love: While you are still feeling the emotions associated with the beliefs, say, "[Name the belief], I release you now with love and with gratitude for your service in my life."

3. **Replace:** Now that the old belief is released, what can I replace it with? Ask yourself the following questions:

What would be possible if...?

Now that I don't believe X, what would I like to be true?

What new belief about myself would give me the outcome that I desire, and what would serve me?

Completing these steps of reflect, release, and replace will program your mind with possibility and set new expectations for yourself, no matter how challenging your situations may be. These three steps will help you update your mindset and prepare for your BFC.

The Words You Say Impact Your Mindset

Pay attention to the words you say when provided with a new opportunity. What got you to this place won't get you to your next destination. Tony Robbins often says that in order to level up, you need to raise your expectations. So, raise them. Expect more of yourself and expect more in your life. Update your mindset to embrace change and go after your BFC.

"Change." That simple word can often trigger negative emotions. Change implies work, and work takes effort and can be hard. Change requires new thoughts, feelings, behaviors, habits, and actions, and we are creatures of habit. Most people are not willing to do the work, but by now we know you are not like most people. Being open to self-development already puts you at an advantage, and reading a book and investing in yourself gives you a head start. Because you want to make a BFC, I know you are not scared of work. You want results. You just haven't had a blueprint for making meaningful change before.

Let's look at change with a new mindset. A mindset that allows growth to occur, possibilities to be explored, and those results to be experienced. For us to embrace change rather than avoid change, it helps to look at the concepts of scarcity versus abundance. Do you see the glass as half full or as half empty? Are you programmed to see what is lacking in your life, or how blessed you are in your life? Don't get me wrong, our brains are wired with a negativity bias, so we need to work extra hard to focus on the positives and on our ability to tap into an abundance mindset.

Simply defined, an abundance mindset is believing there are plenty of resources and opportunities for everyone. A scarcity mindset is believing resources and opportunities are limited. When we have an abundance mindset, we are optimistic and embrace opportunities to learn, grow, and evolve. Adopting an abundance mindset means that you believe there are plenty of opportunities for everyone and that each experience, whether positive or negative, provides us with a chance for growth. As with growth and fixed mindsets, it's possible to have an abundance mindset in some areas of your life and a scarcity mindset in others. The important thing is to notice how you think and where you can expand your mindset.

Just as I once believed I could never be brilliant, we all have limiting beliefs and negative thoughts that we are not even aware of. We have ingrained tendencies that we have learned and developed from our past experiences. Some of these tendencies are protective mechanisms that live in our subconscious minds and automatically hold us back to keep us safe. But what if you could make a Big Freakin' Change and still be safe and actually gain, rather than lose, in the process? You just need a new approach to experience some traction.

I live in Calgary, Alberta, Canada. In the winter, we get a lot of snow, and hitting minus 40 degrees Celsius is no big deal. Sometimes you're pressing the gas pedal, only to find your wheels spinning a groove into the snow beneath them. The only thing that can propel you forward is the very thing that digs you deeper and makes you more stuck. Sometimes all it takes is a change in your approach. Anyone who has spent any time in snowy environments knows that what you need to get out of the snow ruts is more traction. In that situation, you need to put something in front of one of your tires: a stick, some rocks, cardboard, almost anything that can provide you with just a little bit more traction. These little interventions might seem useless. Could a stick that weighs less than a pound really help a car that weighs thousands of pounds? Yes, because all the car needs is a little more traction to gain momentum.

By understanding the nature of the problem, the solution becomes easier. You just need to change your approach and look to your environment for what can help you. My invitation to you is to modify your approach to get unstuck.

A helpful way to tap into thoughts that hold you back is to pay attention to the words you say. Much of our language reveals our mindsets and the limiting beliefs we carry. Paying attention to what you say and replacing the negative words with positive ones can help you adopt growth and abundance mindsets. Notice how your emotional state changes and what starts to show up in your life as you replace negative words with positive words.

Here are few common words and phrases to swap out so you can step into a positive growth and abundance mindset rather than having a negative fixed and scarcity mindset. These positive words are expansive, rather than negative and contracting.

Empowering Word Choices That Shift Your Mindset	
Change is hard	Change is an opportunity to become more of myself
Busy	Full
Tired	Ready for bed
Stressed	Looking forward to resting
Anxious	Excited
Self-help	Self-growth or self-development
Work	Reward
I have to	I get to
Not ready	I'm prepared
Should have	Next time
Not enough	Using what I have
I can't	I choose not to
I have no choice	I am deciding to
Limited	Growing

By updating your mindset and choosing different words, you can start to reframe your perspective and see possibilities instead of problems. Your growth is always waiting outside your comfort zone, and you need to be willing to get uncomfortable. You will never know what's possible unless you try. When I was caught off guard by my friend Amanda calling me brilliant, I had to *reflect* on how I was feeling, *release* the limiting beliefs, and *replace* the language I used. These steps gave me a new point of reference and equipped me to

"Change." That simple word can often trigger negative emotions. **Change implies work, and work takes effort and can be hard.**

step outside my comfort zone. The same is true for my clients and can be true for you.

Courage, Not Confidence

One of my coaching clients, Janessa, came to me because she was feeling stuck in her professional and personal life. She was stressed out trying to launch her new real estate business. She wanted to expand into new locations, invest in marketing, develop software technology, and manage all of the day-to-day operations. She needed to land clients to generate cash flow and prove her business model, but the stress of a start-up was consuming her. She was stuck in a scarcity mindset.

I could have jumped in and focused on her business activities, but I have learned that there is always a connection between how fast and far entrepreneurs go in business and how positive and expansive their mindsets are. The same is true when dealing with life situations. I always try to identify how my clients are stuck in a fixed mindset and how I can help them shift their mindset with curiosity.

We did an exercise to update her mindset in preparation for her business launch. I knew that if she was undertaking change, her mindset needed to be new to carry her forward with the belief it was possible. So, we went through the three-step process of reflect, release, and replace.

Reflect: I asked Janessa to think about where she currently was and what her insecurities and emotions were. She said she was feeling scared her business might not work.

Release: I invited her to decide what she would like to think instead. I invited her to make the decision to release the doubt generated by a previous failed business and to remind herself it was okay to take on risk.

Replace: She needed to remove the fear of failure and replace it with a belief in herself and who she wanted to become as a CEO. She wrote it down and said it out loud to bring her new mindset to life. I reminded her she would feel ready later.

Janessa worked on her mindset and did this exercise daily, and even though she did not yet truly believe it, her business started to come together, and she landed clients right away. She could not believe the connection between her mindset and the momentum in her business. She told me she thought it was a bit woo-woo, but after trying it, she had become a firm believer in the connection between mindset and momentum. This was a great win for her, but mindset updates are not a one-and-done task. As we uplevel, we need to keep leveling up. New fears came to the surface for Janessa, which we then addressed. She was worried about being a good mom and running a business, and she worried about the number of hours required to build a big business. She was focusing on problems and living in fear. We addressed her fears and limiting beliefs and went through the process again.

A few weeks after her launch, Janessa called me in tears. "I am so frustrated. I am not getting the results I projected."

Constantly craving results is normal for type A personalities, high achievers, people with high expectations, and entrepreneurs. Instead of challenging her, I needed to switch her mindset into a positive one so she could start seeing possibilities again, rather than only staring at the problems. She needed to flip the script in her mind to see abundance and opportunity, rather than scarcity and limitations. She was focused on everything that was lacking in her business: what was not good enough, not ready enough, and not polished enough.

"What is one thing that would be amazing for your business that you don't think is possible now?" I asked her later in person. "Let's think big, massive!" I wanted her to have a moment of reflection about what was possible beyond the limits of her current mindset.

She thought about it as she looked at me as if I was crazy and sighed out loud.

"If I could wave a magic wand and grant you a wish for your business, what would you want right now?" I said.

Her face softened as she looked at me. "I would love to interview this multibillionaire in the banking and real estate industry to ask him about my business model," she said, then laughed out loud as if that were impossible. "It would be amazing to have his vote of confidence, to know that my business model is viable—or even brilliant."

"How can we do this?" I asked.

"Well, it probably would never happen."

She wanted to wait for everything to be perfectly in place before she would take action. As I brainstormed ways we could get in touch with him, she rolled her eyes at me in disbelief that I was even considering it.

"You think that you can make that happen?" she said.

"What if it is possible?" I asked. Then in my "dance teacher" voice, I added, "Let's make it possible."

Janessa was caught in the problems. I wanted to get her into a growth mindset and revisit what else was possible. When we live in fear, it's hard to see possibilities.

As Janessa and I brainstormed ideas, we landed on one that could work. It was a long shot but possible. "Create a video where you introduce yourself," I said to her with conviction, "what you know of his business, your business model, and the impact you want to make. Ask for twenty minutes of his time and see where that takes you."

This approach would require minimal effort and some mental energy, but no money, and the reward if successful could be significant for her. I wanted her to see that taking some risk was okay. Sure, she could get rejected and waste some time, or she could get the opportunity she wanted, which would move her forward in a massive way. Regardless of the result, taking this step would update her mindset to dream bigger, beyond what she even thought was possible. This is the power of taking a chance and putting yourself out there: your mental endurance increases, and you become less scared of taking risks. The reward of taking a chance, no matter what the outcome is, is confidence. When you take a chance on yourself, increase your risk, and become vulnerable, you develop your confidence.

Janessa started to sweat, and her chest became splotchy.

"It's okay to take on risk without feeling ready," I said with a smile.

Though she felt she was not ready and assumed her business model wasn't polished enough, her script wasn't refined enough, and she wasn't good enough, she shot the video. She didn't have the best LinkedIn account or a good enough camera—more obstacles for her to overcome—but she had the courage to shoot the video. After a few takes and rounds of feedback and edits, she had a plan.

The first step in the process was deciding that it was *possible* to reach out to the billionaire. Her internal dialogue shifted from feeling doubtful of her abilities to realizing her potential. When we talk through the possible scenarios of getting rejected or getting accepted, we realize that often what we fear is far worse than what would actually happen.

I reminded her, and I remind you, that there is never a perfect time or perfect situation to make the change you truly desire, but there is a perfect way to make it happen. It's by taking action and believing in your ability. Janessa gained the momentum to tackle the obstacles that came up. She stopped self-doubt from flooding her completely as she stepped out of limiting beliefs into a larger landscape of possibility.

It was a Thursday night at 7 p.m. when I received this text message from Janessa: "OMG, I did it."

She had sent off the video to Mr. Billionaire and was anxiously waiting for a reply and doubting she would get one. She assumed it would take days before she heard back from him, if at all. To her surprise, she checked her phone before she went to bed, and she had a reply!

"Hi Janessa," he replied. "I am happy to meet with you. My assistant will send you an invite."

She called me with excitement and said she could not believe she even got a reply—and so quickly, and he said *yes*! She had released what she thought was never possible and replaced it with possibility. She released the fixed mindset she had been carrying, and she stepped into a growth mindset. It paid off.

"Woohoo! This is what I am talking about," I said, as I fist-pumped the air.

Everything shifted in that one moment of experiencing a significant win that she'd thought was not even remotely possible. This was her reset and update. She reset her mind to look for possibilities and to believe in abundance.

After she had her virtual meeting with him, she got her energy back, her passion returned, and she found her determination again. Just getting a response validated her feeling of worthiness. She had stepped out of her comfort zone, took a risk, and received a reward. Was it uncomfortable? Yes. Was it worth it? *Hell yes!* Where do you need to step out and ask for something?

Janessa found the courage to be different and the courage to ask. So many women have big ideas and goals, but we lack the confidence to pursue them. It starts with thinking big and reframing the way we think about risk. You don't need to feel ready; you can take on risk, and know it's okay to fail. I have been rejected several times, but I have learned it is just part of the process when you level up.

Mr. Billionaire told Janessa how people are reaching out to him and asking for his time daily. However, because she was different and sent a video and put some intentional effort into the ask, it stood out to him, and he agreed to meet with her. When you follow protocol and do it exactly like everyone else, you blend in; you don't stand out. Tell yourself you are brilliant and look for possibilities. It's okay to deviate from what you "should" do. Be different. Be bold. Be brilliant. Be you. No one can be a better you than you. When you really understand this truth, you realize competing against others is irrelevant and you only need to pay attention to who you were and who you are becoming.

Blown away by the experience, Janessa got busy working on the feedback she received. Her mind expanded to think even bigger, so she took on bigger risks by adding diverse strategic partnerships, joining new podcasts, and making bolder decisions with her rates, policies, and procedures. With the simple thought of "I wonder what else is possible," she got out of her fixed mindset and adopted a growth mindset. With this mindset update, everything changed in her business and her life. She hired a nanny and even took a two-week holiday. When the mind expands, our life expands too. Updating your mindset is the best way to tap into possibilities.

We usually start by playing small, in the confining zone of possibility, out of fear. That's where most people stop. The act of starting is the hardest, so once you start, keep moving forward. Entrepreneurship and life are about managing problems and making decisions. Our minds are wired to see the negative, so we need to work extra hard to focus on the positives and the possibilities. Remember this when you step out: you'll identify the possible negatives but recognize the possible positives too. When we step out of our comfort zone and don't allow fear to hold us back, we step into possibility. Opportunity lies outside our comfort zones. To reach possibility and opportunity, you have to step out and plant your seed of possibility.

You may be thinking there is no way you could ever do something like what Janessa did because you are not confident enough. Let me be clear, what I asked Janessa to do required courage, not confidence. She was not feeling confident at all. She was stuck feeling insecure about her life and business, as she juggled motherhood and entrepreneurship. She could only see her problems, and she never considered she would actually reach out to Mr. Billionaire to pick his brilliant brain. Talking to him was intimidating, but after she did it, she felt like she could talk to anyone. Her mindset expanded exponentially after she took a big step outside her comfort zone.

Janessa needed to flip the script: she moved from self-doubt and feeling not good enough or ready enough to knowing she was good enough and her business model was too. She changed her focus from problems and limited resources to possibilities and abundance.

When we're deciding to make a Big Freakin' Change, we question our ability and decisions simply because we lack experience. It's new, exciting, and simultaneously scary. Those feelings are a good sign to move forward, not a reason to hold you back. Feelings of insecurity and overwhelm are part of updating your mindset; you will be less fearful next time. And just in case you are wondering, the best day to go after anything you want is today! Stop regretting that you haven't done the thing yet, or beating yourself up with the "should have, would have, could have," and start the process of your BFC.

Maybe You're Brilliant

Everything you carry in your mind takes up space. The long to-do list, the limiting beliefs, the self-judgment, and the self-criticism. Like Janessa, many of us have automatic negative thoughts, and we need to make space for positive ones. With an abundance mindset, you consciously choose to see possibilities rather than problems. You shift from feeling discouraged to feeling determined, and you are more likely to say yes to life. When you say yes to life, life says yes back to you, and it has your back. God, the Universe, Karma, whatever you believe in believes in you.

Just imagine what you would do and how you would behave if everyone always told you that you were brilliant and, more importantly, you felt it? My guess is you would make bigger and bolder decisions, take on more risk, and feel more confident. You would trust yourself and your abilities, and you would feel better in your mind, body, and soul. You would become more of the person you were meant to be with belief in yourself.

And just in case no one has ever told you that you are brilliant, let me do it for you now: You. Are. Brilliant!

 Hand on Heart

Affirm yourself and say this out loud:

In order to update my mindset and embrace the next version of myself, I give myself permission to let go of judgment of myself, others, and my life. I am embracing change and giving myself the opportunity to think differently so that I can live differently. I am choosing to think differently to achieve different results in my life.

Place your hand on your heart and take a few deep breaths.

Take a moment to think about what is really holding you back and what part of your mindset needs to be updated first. Without overanalyzing or thinking too much about it, write down what pops into your mind first, without judgment and only with love:

What is my greatest insecurity?

What would my life look like if that was removed?

What is my wildest dream, and how can I take a step toward it?

Who do I want to become?

How do I want to feel as I step into this next version of myself?

How would I describe the next version of myself?

What would my ninety-year-old self say to me right now about these reflections?

P.S. When you bring your mindset into alignment with a new version of yourself, change will feel consistent with who you are becoming. A new mindset can feel fragile at first, but with reinforcement, it will become strong, and it will support you on your journey.

5
SMALL STEPS, MASSIVE CHANGE

*"To improve is to change,
so to be perfect is to have changed often."*

WINSTON CHURCHILL

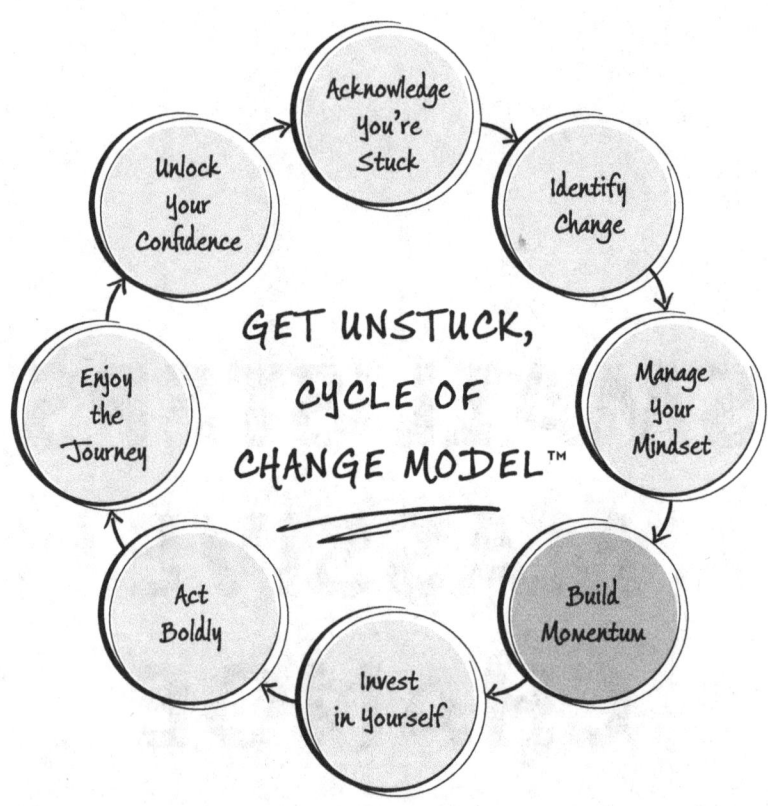

After acknowledging you were stuck, you identified the type of change you wanted to make and updated your mindset. You are now focusing on behavioral changes to build momentum. Building momentum means making small changes within your comfort zone.

WAS APPROACHING graduation from the University of Calgary with a degree in business, majoring in marketing, and a degree in fine arts, majoring in psychology. My degrees were considered an odd combination in 2006 but are common now. Sometimes what is considered odd can be a signal that we are one of the first to do something. Dr. Proudfoot, my strategic management professor, came up to me and handed me a piece of paper. "Cara, a job posting just came across my desk that you would be perfect for! You should apply."

He was one of my favorite professors, and I respected his opinion. The fact that he took the time to encourage me felt good, and I read the job description with excitement.

"Investor relations manager. Wow! I like the way that sounds!"

The description mentioned the importance of creativity in the job. "No problem there. I'm a dancer! Check!" I had spent the last sixteen years exercising my creative muscle as a dancer and choreographer. I felt more at home in that creative zone than anywhere else.

The position also required strong strategic thinking skills. Overcoming learning disabilities to graduate with a double bachelor's degree required strategy, and I had learned to love it. "Check!" I thought as I ticked another imaginary box on a "perfect for me" list.

I could see why Dr. Proudfoot recommended that I apply for the job. It felt as if it was tailor-made for me with each of my strengths in mind. I started to imagine myself in the role, working with investors and building a successful career in a lucrative industry. Getting this job would most certainly fast-track my career.

Near the end of the description, I came to the educational requirements and my emerging fantasy of becoming a successful investor relations manager evaporated.

MBA—master of business administration.

My budding confidence sank as quickly as it had arisen.

"Ugh. I should have known better! Who am I to think I could qualify for such an incredible job just out of university? I don't even have any experience in this industry."

I read the job description again, and the second time, I noticed that I didn't meet quite a few of the required qualifications. A few of them I didn't even *understand*. How had I missed those the first time?

Within minutes, I'd gone from confident and excited to dejected and self-critical.

Walking away, I crumpled up the paper and was about to toss it in a garbage bin when a voice inside me whispered, "What *if*, Cara?" I could have ignored the voice, but I had learned to listen to my intuition over the years. So I leaned in.

Hmmm...

What. If.

What if my soft skills *were* enough to make me perfect for the job? I could learn the hard skills, couldn't I?

What *if* what Dr. Proudfoot saw in me *was* enough to not only get the job but succeed at it? He did know me, after all, and he was an accomplished professional.

What if I *could* get the job? It would be a fantastic start to my career. What did I have to lose anyway? I knew men applied for jobs without meeting all of the criteria, so maybe, just maybe, I could too.

Planting a Seed of Possibility

A seed of possibility was all I needed in that moment. I decided to push back against fear for just long enough to take one step toward the dream of getting this job.

Actually getting the job still seemed unrealistic, with all the requirements that I didn't meet printed in black and white before my eyes. However, I also realized that success comes in different shapes and forms.

"They may not hire me. They may not interview me. Heck, they may not even read my résumé. But success for me right now is just taking the next step. I don't have control over their response, but I do have control over how I choose to show up."

For the past year, I had developed a daily habit of working on my mindset, and this redefinition of success, and the tiny boost of confidence it gave me, was the result. I decided to lean into possibility and take the first small step of writing my résumé and submitting it. I knew that, no matter what, I could successfully complete that step and I could take pride in the way I showed up for myself.

I spent the entire next day working on my résumé, tailoring it to showcase my unique skills with their specific requirements. It was as much a masterpiece as a résumé could be, and I was proud of myself for taking that step. I sent it with a personalized cover letter, trying to stand out from the crowd.

Even without knowing how they would respond, or even *if* they would respond, I felt a growing confidence, as if I was moving in the right direction. In the right direction of the job, but also the right direction in my life. If I didn't get the job, at least my résumé was updated, and that was a win. More importantly, I showed up for myself, and that alone was a success.

Two weeks passed, each day a blur of constantly checking my email and voicemail for a reply, with not so much as a "Thank you for your application" to show for it. I'd settled into the reality that I wasn't qualified enough for the job, so I was surprised when the phone rang and on the other end was an invitation to come in for an interview. They had reviewed my résumé and were "really interested" to meet me in person.

A flutter of excitement rose and then gave way to a flutter of fear. "What do I do now?" I thought. Over the past two weeks, I'd considered how much more qualified other candidates must be, and I didn't know how I would measure up.

But what I realized when I submitted my résumé was that I didn't need to know everything. I just needed to know the next right step.

Even if I didn't get the job in the end, I could successfully complete a number of small steps and build a habit of success. Becoming successful includes building new habits of discipline and consistency and keeping your word to yourself.

So I made a commitment to build my confidence every day by looking in the mirror and telling myself that I was born for this, that I was the best candidate, that I had superpowers that would make me succeed. If I wanted them to believe in me, I had to believe in me. No one would believe in me more than me. And I kept that commitment. It felt silly at first, but I needed to do it so I could feel it and then believe it.

I decided the next right step was to go shopping. I bought a *killer* outfit. Bright pink blouse, white blazer, gold hoop earrings. I was going to look the part—and stand out.

I researched the company and spoke with someone on their team who I knew from university classes. I became familiar with their culture, their priorities, and their leadership team. I prepared my responses to common questions and practiced delivering my responses aloud.

Every day I was stretching my limits, slowly moving my "next small steps" to the very edge of my comfort zone. Each time I completed a step, and the promise I had made to myself to complete it, I rewarded myself with a fist pump celebration and a one-person dance party. I didn't know it then, but I was building momentum toward getting this job by creating a habit of success and stepping into the energy of it.

The day of the interview finally came. I'd be lying if I didn't admit to feeling nervous, but I also felt the comforting warmth of confidence that came from showing up for myself day after day. Despite the fact that I didn't qualify on paper, I felt like I had qualified myself.

"Cara? I'm Brad. It's nice to meet you. Come on into my office." My interviewer surprised me with his warmth as he extended his hand toward mine. I had been practicing my handshake and gave him a firm squeeze with two shakes, smiled, and looked him directly in the eyes.

We sat down, and the interview began. But in my mind, the interview had begun the moment I listened to the inner voice asking me,

"What if?" In my mind, the interview had continued every day since then as I took small step after small step toward this job.

I asked him, "What does the ideal candidate look like for you?"

He seemed impressed with the question and mentioned that no one had ever asked him that before. I listened carefully to every word he said. I wanted to be strategic with my responses to showcase the qualities he was looking for in my answers. I didn't know much about the industry, but I had done my research and had an answer for every question he asked. Most of his questions I had anticipated and prepared for. I had taken an interviewing preparation session in university, which helped me understand how to deliver the answers they were looking for while keeping in mind how he defined the ideal candidate.

I noticed his energy shift from curious to impressed; he smiled more, nodded his head, and raised his eyebrows at my answers. He was leaning toward me across from the desk and seemed pleased.

"Well, Cara, on paper you don't meet several of our criteria for the position." My heart sank. He continued, "But I like your attitude and the way you show up. On top of that, you were clearly well prepared for our interview today. This is exactly the kind of attitude and approach we need in this position, and I think you would do a great job."

I sat there unsure of what he would say next. Was he interested in hiring me, or was this a nice way to say, "You're not qualified"? And then he asked me, "What are your salary expectations?"

In all my preparation for this interview, this was the one aspect I hadn't even considered. I knew the position paid well, but I hadn't thought to consider what my expectations should be. Should I ask on the low end of the salary range because of my lack of experience? Should I ask on the high end to show him that I'm confident?

Flustered for a minute, I calmed myself, looked him dead in the eyes, and said in the most confident voice I could muster, "I want to be paid for the value I bring, and I know you will give me a fair offer." This sentence came out of me then almost as if my higher self stepped in and took over for a moment, and now I use it to help people prepare for the compensation question in interviews if they are unsure of what's a reasonable ask.

Brad smiled. "Okay, Cara. Then as a next step, I'd like you to prepare a case study of one of our clients and submit it to me by email in a week."

"Thank you, Brad," I replied. "I've brought a few case studies I completed in university." I handed him a folder. "Is this what you are looking for?"

He looked stunned for a moment and then laughed as he thumbed through my case folder skimming through the files. "Yes, Cara. This is *exactly* what I'm looking for. I would like to confirm you for the next round of interviews."

I barely remember what happened next. I do have a vague memory that I didn't so much *walk* out of that office, as I did *float*. It felt like I had been offered the job even though it was only the next round of interviews. I had put myself out there and learned it was safe to take a risk and succeed. I showed up as myself, big hoop earrings and all. My preparation worked. My mindset moved me forward, and I did it. Through two more interviews, bouncing between feeling insecure and confident, I kept going. One step at a time.

I painted the picture of what success would look like and kept focusing on the step ahead of me. During the following rounds, I felt intimidated waiting with male candidates in their fancy pin-striped suits, but I reminded myself to stay the course. I sat up tall and breathed deeply. I took a moment to work backward and see the steps involved, to identify the stepping stones and to redefine success as the completion of the next small step.

And finally, I got an email with the subject line "Offer."

Wow, I've never fist-pumped the air so hard.

One of my favorite ways to celebrate was to go to Dairy Queen and buy myself a small Skor Blizzard. That moment certainly met the criteria for celebration. I went straight to Dairy Queen and ordered a large one. As I savored each bite, letting the ice cream melt in my mouth, I reflected on the process and celebrated not only the final outcome but all the little outcomes along the way. I had chosen to lean into possibility, instead of staying stuck in fear.

I had developed a habit of success by taking small steps and being committed to them. Those small steps gave me confidence and momentum, and that momentum carried me into this big and exciting opportunity. I proved to myself that I could do whatever I wanted if I was willing to be courageous and do the work. And you can too. Put yourself out there, prepare, plan, execute, build momentum, ask questions, stay the course, and trust yourself.

Every big change is a series of small steps. The path to successfully making change depends on our ability to complete the small steps along the way. If you don't take the first step, you never know how far you could have gone, you never know what is possible for you, and you never learn the important lesson of trusting yourself.

We often look at other people's success and fail to realize what it took them to get there. Nobody understands a journey they have not walked. We see the results and think it happened magically or the path was easy. We underestimate the work required for a big change. BFCs require hard work and vulnerability. I went from a student to an investor relations manager, a working professional. Each step along the way was hard. Each step was necessary. Each step was rewarding.

The key to making the change that you'd like in your life is to focus on momentum, trusting that the outcome will follow. The way to build momentum is to start with small, manageable steps that are within your zone of optimal change. Then celebrate your success, however small, before moving on to the next small, manageable step. Celebrate often so your mind looks for more ways to win. Over time, you will develop a deeper trust in yourself and have more confidence to make bigger changes in the future.

Don't Disqualify Yourself Early

When we want to make change and take on risk, we can often come up with reasons not to do so. Our minds tell us we are not good enough, ready enough, or prepared enough to keep us safe. We disqualify ourselves all the time, sometimes before we take the first necessary step to a BFC. I could have disqualified myself by not even applying, assuming that someone else was better for the position than me.

When we do decide to move forward and step into action, we often get persuaded to give up early. Especially when it gets hard. We justify why we should not continue the journey when challenges arise. We let fear win. We look for reasons why we don't measure up. Starting anything is easy; finishing is hard. What happens in the middle makes all the difference. Here's what I know: don't disqualify yourself until you get disqualified.

When we step into action with a growth mindset, there will always be a space between who we are and who we want to become. That is the journey. This is where learning happens. This is how growth occurs. When the gap between an opportunity and what we feel ready or qualified to do is massive, it's easier to bridge that gap by focusing on one small step at a time. I had to focus on each step, not the destination, in the job application process because getting the job was intimidating and too far out of reach for me to focus on. Yes, waiting was part of the process. I wanted to give up many times, but I reminded myself not to disqualify myself when fear got a grip on me.

We need to continue to take the next steps until the process ends or we get disqualified, not before that point. It will get hard. Hard is part of the game. Hard challenges you. Hard expands you. Hard teaches you. So, no matter the outcome, you win if you make the decision to stay in the game of change.

I knew if I prepared to the best of my ability, I would feel proud of myself even if I did not get the job. If I took shortcuts or cut corners, I would always wonder, "What if?" When we are in a zone of possibility and fear greets us, we can manage it by preparing ourselves to the best of our ability and following our course step by step. Giving up early only hurts our confidence levels. We think we are doing ourselves a favor, but we are actually damaging our self-esteem as we failed to keep our word to ourselves.

Most things are manageable one step at a time. Small steps add up to massive changes. By taking one small step forward, you can change the trajectory of your life forever. One application at a time, one interview at a time, one opportunity at a time. When you get out

Here's what I know: **don't disqualify yourself until you get disqualified.**

of your head, embrace fear, and step into action, life happens, and you develop your confidence. Things often make sense only in hindsight, so keep looking forward and move forward one step at a time.

Don't Start with the Big Things

So many of us get stuck in overwhelm when making change, but that doesn't have to be the case. By taking small steps, we are more likely to create positive momentum and build our confidence along the way.

When we're desperate for change, we tend to set massive goals. We have all heard the phrase "Go big or go home," which reflects all-or-nothing thinking. I like to think, "Go small and stand tall," knowing the habit of success will stack up. When the gap between where we are and where we want to go is so wide, it discourages and often defeats us. Let's be real: big-picture goals usually only work for the minority of highly disciplined and self-motivated people. If this is you, fist pump and high five to you. Unfortunately, most of us are more familiar with failure than victory when we've set big goals. We start strong and over time lose our momentum, especially when we don't see results as quickly as we would like. When the actions taken are too drastic, it's difficult to sustain them.

When the gap between where you are and where you want to go is massive, your brain cannot even begin to imagine, adapt, or comprehend the needed change. When we want the instant gratification of a big change, we throw ourselves into the deep end without knowing how to swim. Making small shifts over time can lead to massive change; instead of sinking, you start to swim. We need vision and execution to move from our mindset into action with small steps that are attainable and sustainable.

James Clear, author of *Atomic Habits*, pulls from biology, psychology, and neuroscience to provide simple and effective ways to make habits stick. He suggests that if we get just 1 percent better every day, we will become thirty-seven times better after one year. This is both massive change and doable. On the contrary, if you get 1 percent worse each day for a year, you decline nearly to zero, which is extremely discouraging. The compound effect of small shifts in either direction is huge.

Clear focuses on how "tiny changes" create "remarkable results." He identifies habits, decision making, and continuous improvement as key areas of change. Consider how you would feel if you were focused on making continual improvements, rather than on instant gratification or massive gains. Most likely, you would feel encouraged, motivated, and bolstered by a few early wins that keep you moving forward. Wins set us up for success by giving us momentum.

When striving to make any behavior change, Clear suggests these four rules to make it stick:

1. Make it obvious.
2. Make it attractive.
3. Make it easy.
4. Make it satisfying.

When you want to make significant change, it's imperative that you get clear on what you want, identify the benefits the change will provide you with, make it attainable and achievable, and set yourself up for success by making it positive and rewarding. Any type of change, small or large, can be hard. Make it easier on yourself by making changes small, gradual, and continual. Remember to keep taking small steps, no matter how insignificant or small you may think they are, because they all add up.

Small Shifts Add Up to Big Changes

When I think about what small shifts that add up to big changes look like, I think back to the first group of women I taught hip-hop dance to when I opened my studio at twenty-seven years old. Moms of children taking dance would often tell me that they would love to learn how to dance, but they were waiting until they felt ready before they joined the class.

This is typical for most of us, and it's completely backward. We want to do something, but we lack the skill; without taking any kind of action, we think one day we will feel ready. It's one thing to think about doing something and another to do it. This is what it means to move out of mindset into action. You need to take action to change the way you think, one small step at a time. For those women, that first step was signing up.

Over the past fifteen years, I have had people from all walks of life take classes. Our bodies were made to move, and I love inspiring women to move them; it brings a form of connection to the soul that only movement can offer. I've had young single women, married women, divorced women, moms, and former dancers as students. They all come for different reasons but leave feeling more comfortable in their own skin and more confident than when they first arrived. There was a schoolteacher, accountant, engineer, librarian, Starbucks barista, massage therapist, stay-at-home mom, and university student. Some came to feel more confident, others to have fun, some to get a good workout, to get out of the house, or to have some time just for themselves. They all wanted to learn how to dance.

What they didn't recognize was that all of them needed to shift their mindsets into action and take time to connect with themselves. Connection to oneself is often underrated and overlooked; life gets busy for all of us. That connection to themselves was the missing key to unlock their confidence, feel comfortable in their bodies, and step into courage in their lives. Dance is not only about learning dance steps. It's also about showing up for yourself and giving yourself permission to be seen, which goes far beyond the studio walls into all aspects of life. I have never met a woman who doesn't wish she had more confidence in some area of life. Connecting with ourselves gives us this invaluable gift and momentum like no other. Sadly, it's not obvious that we've lost connection with ourselves until we are in a rut, desperate to get out.

"Welcome everyone, my name is Cara," I announced at the start of that first hip-hop class. "I am proud of you for showing up." I could tell from their lack of eye contact, awkward stances, and crossed arms that they were all nervous. "I know it's hard trying something new, and I know you can feel vulnerable learning anything new."

A few of them sighed out loud and uncrossed their arms in relief, as I validated how they were feeling.

"You already did the hardest part and showed up. You have courage," I said. I wanted their mindsets to shift from fear to pride.

A few ladies' shoulders dropped.

"I will take care of the rest," I said with a smile.

A few more of them relaxed and started to breathe again. They needed to know they were normal and what they were feeling was normal. Far too often, we think we are the only ones that sit in fear when we want to try something new, unaware that others are feeling the same thing. We can't understand what's going on inside others when we only have access to their outsides.

I put on some hip-hop beats that were high energy, and we started with a good old step-touch. I taught them the beat of the music. I made them clap. I praised them for how good they were as I taught them within their comfort zone, stretching them ever so slightly.

"Ladies, get your eyes off the floor," I said, looking through the mirror, smiling at them.

A few of them looked around, a few looked up, and only a couple looked at themselves. I then turned off the music and stopped the class.

"Ladies, I want you to know that you will learn how to dance. It's time to look at yourself and connect back with your body. No more looking at the floor. Look at yourself. Just let yourself be. Give yourself permission to let loose, and the dance moves will come."

A few of them looked at their reflection in the mirror, uncomfortable and vulnerable but with a sliver of connection. I wanted them to take a moment to look at themselves in the mirror. To really see themselves as they were in that moment. Beautiful, bold, and brave. Not to be comparing themselves with others to see how they measure up or to feel inadequate, but to take a moment and just be. To be in their bodies and to celebrate themselves regardless of their skill set, coordination, or body size. Those were the first steps before learning how to move. The truth was they were more similar than they were different. Their fears, their hopes, their insecurities, and everything on their minds were similar. Everyone assumes they are the only one with fears, but everyone has them. We just don't talk about them, and we disguise them in different ways.

After some more encouragement, they all were looking at themselves in the mirror, which grew more comfortable for them over time. Some even smiled and started performing with their faces, giving themselves permission to feel joy. They took a minute to celebrate themselves—first for showing up and second for brushing up against the edges of their comfort zones and then stepping out of their comfort zones. It wasn't about how well they could dance; it was about celebrating their wins one dance step at a time. I knew if they could feel like they were winning, they would keep coming. If they felt inadequate, they would quit and give up. I didn't want anyone to give up on themselves. This is how simple small wins add up to significant big changes.

They were no longer looking at each other, scared of judgment or stuck in comparison; they were present, in their bodies, and looking at themselves. They were connected. They got out of their heads and into their bodies through action. They had gained momentum by taking little steps that added up to create a full routine.

We repeated each step over and over to build their confidence and celebrate it. Each week, the ladies became more comfortable and even started showing up early to chat with each other. They were eager to learn because they were no longer overthinking; they were in the act of being.

Divina, the librarian, was sure she could never find the beat even if her life depended on it. She was always off beat, and her frustration increased. It seemed as if the harder she focused on it, the worse she got. I told her to stop thinking about it for that week, that the beat would come.

The next week, she came in and was eager to get to the front row for warmup. She was beaming. "I found the beat!" she exclaimed. Divina was thrilled to show all of us her step-touch to the beat of the music. The ladies cheered loudly for her. She had found her groove after she found the beat. Her eyes came off the floor, and she smiled at herself, amazed she was dancing to the beat. She no longer stood in the back corner scared to be seen. She had momentum. Divina could not believe how much more comfortable she felt, and that allowed her to show up bigger than she thought was possible and dance harder than she knew she could.

Over the course of three months, I saw something profound happen to each of the ladies at different moments. Their energy expanded, and they took up more space than they did when they first joined the class. They stood taller and had better posture. The room also felt lighter. Insecurities were pushed to the sidelines, and courage and confidence were brought to the center. They laughed with each other, they celebrated each other, and they helped each other master the steps.

What really happened was that they all connected with themselves first, which was a vital relationship they had lost for years, and that gave them momentum to connect with others. They felt their own presences again, appreciated who they were, challenged their mindsets, and embraced their bodies; they all found their groove. And when this happened, they started wearing more form-fitting clothes; some even bought new outfits, feeling proud of their bodies. They felt good again. They looked at themselves and liked what they saw. The ladies in my dance class became more themselves. They stopped hiding and started shining. They stepped into their brilliance.

It's through the small steps that we learn to find comfort in who we are. It's in taking a moment to feel the beat of the music and the beat in our heart that we connect to ourselves. It's in stretching and flexing that we become more comfortable in and with ourselves. When we are more comfortable with who we are and how we show up, we connect better to others and take bigger chances in life. All of the ladies learned to dance, and more importantly, they learned to trust themselves to step into action in their lives, one step at a time. This is how momentum is built: over time by taking one small step at a time. Just as in dance, we put steps together to make beautiful choreography. In life, the steps come together to make a masterpiece.

**When you get
out of your head,
embrace fear, and
step into action,
you develop
your confidence.**

After our class ended, their confidence expanded to other areas of their lives. Carol started working out again, carving out a little time to herself each day. Nicolette bought some new clothes and didn't feel guilty about it. Marina started dating again with less fear about being rejected, and Susan planned a date with her husband, feeling more like herself again. Those are the kinds of impacts confidence can have on our lives. When we experience confidence in one area, it moves the needle in other areas. We expand. Life expands. Everything changes. We change. The most beautiful part of change is it teaches others that they too can make change.

Years later, I ran into Jenna, the doctor, who was highly conservative and introverted and who had hated looking at herself in the mirror.

"Wow, you look great, Jenna!" I said. I couldn't quite put my finger on what had changed, but her energy and essence had awakened. Her eyes were sparkling, and she seemed lighter and looked younger.

She smiled at me and said, "I remind myself each morning that it's okay to be seen and take chances. I show up for myself now. Dance taught me that."

I hugged her tight. "I am so proud of you."

When we try something new and succeed, that action creates confidence in other areas of our life too. Sometimes it happens instantly, and other times we see the impact later. Embracing your fear, tapping into your courage, and finding your confidence always pay off in spades.

The Power of Celebrating Wins

When we don't feel ready to sign up for the dance class, buy the new clothes, apply for the job, join the dating site, or run the marathon, it can be helpful to work backward to understand what you *really* want to experience. Getting specific on the feeling clears the path to your goal and keeps you focused and motivated in the process. When you imagine all the details—how you want to feel, what you want to do, and who you want to become—you can see the way forward and are more likely to continue and pick up some momentum.

Sometimes, we get so caught up in our day-to-day lives that we don't take time to dream about where we would like to go and what's possible. Working backward provides clarity and confidence to persist when things get challenging, because we can see the next steps involved.

During the job interview process I described to you earlier, I visualized what it would be like to be in a boardroom making a presentation, and how that would feel, and that exercise helped me take the next right step and acknowledge the progress I'd made so far. So often, we only see how far we still have to go, and we forget to see how far we have come. When you gain traction, you have an opportunity to celebrate your wins, which will encourage you to keep going. Every win in your life, regardless of its size, is worth celebrating, because *you* are worth celebrating. What you focus on expands; when you focus on the wins in your life, you create and see more wins in your life.

Celebrating programs your mind to look for more wins and to lean into them, creating a habit of winning. This may feel a bit foreign at first, as we tend to shy away from celebrating wins, especially as women. Some of us think it is similar to bragging and we don't want to make others feel uncomfortable, but it might just be that *we* are uncomfortable because we lack experience celebrating. It's easier to have pity parties than success celebrations. As much as we want success, it can feel uncomfortable when we experience it. We first need to realize we are worthy of celebrating our wins and then celebrate them.

We wear exhaustion as a brooch of honor and tuck wins away deep in our pockets. Imagine how our energy would expand if we celebrated more than complained, if we talked about concepts and dreams rather than people and problems, and if we dreamed bigger while awake rather than craving more sleep at night. Well, I know for myself life would feel lighter, and more women would rise up not only for themselves but to help others rise along the way. This won't happen overnight, but it can happen by celebrating each other more often so we all gain experience and know it's okay to win and it's okay to rise.

There is science that supports celebrating wins too. When we take time to celebrate, we get to enjoy the feeling of accomplishment, and that feeling programs our minds to look for what else might be possible. It activates the "reward circuit" in the brain called the limbic system. The reward circuit links together brain structures that control and regulate our ability to feel pleasure. Pleasure motivates us to repeat behaviors. This is a good thing, so bring on the wins, ladies, and celebrate them, as doing so will motivate you to take a risk again! Remember we are wired with a negative default. Celebrating wins programs your mind, body, and soul for what success feels like. This is a win in itself! By intentionally noticing what is going *right* in your life, we make room for more things to go right in the future. Celebrating also inspires and encourages others that they too can succeed.

Your brain can only pay attention to and retain so much information at any given time, so focusing on wins helps you win more often. There is a part of your brain, the prefrontal cortex, that is responsible for filtering information. It serves as a control center that mediates our highest cognitive abilities, such as concentration, planning, decision making, insight, judgment, and memory retrieval. This is the mechanism behind why what you focus on truly does expand.

Author of *The Gap and the Gain* and strategic coach Dan Sullivan writes, "Your future growth and progress are now based in your understanding about the difference between the two ways in which you can measure yourself: against the ideal, which puts you in what I call 'The Gap,' and against your starting point, which puts you in 'The Gain,' appreciating all that you've accomplished." I say focus on the gain. It will help you move forward, and let's face it, there will always be people ahead of you, so focus on *your* growth.

Prospect theory suggests that people strongly prefer avoiding losses over acquiring gains. This loss aversion is so strong that it can lead to negativity bias. Loss aversion is a cognitive bias describing that the pain of losing is twice as powerful as the pleasure of gaining. As an example, it feels better not to lose one hundred dollars than to find one hundred dollars. We don't like losing, and that prevents us from trying. We don't take on risks, fearing we will experience loss. We are more fearful about losing than we are excited to win. This is part of what makes celebrating wins so powerful.

Momentum Creates More Momentum

There can be obstacles standing in our way or a flowing force moving us forward with momentum. When we think of making a BFC, we need courage to step forward, and we want to feel positive, proud, powerful, and brave. We want to move away from feeling overwhelmed, powerless, anxious, or stressed out, as these are fear-based emotions that slow us down. Here are a few more opposing emotions to pay attention to, so you can keep moving forward with the motivation to keep stepping out:

- Overwhelm versus calm
- Discouragement versus encouragement
- Failure versus success
- Distrust versus trust in ourselves
- Obsessing over losses versus celebrating wins
- Overthinking in our mind versus trusting our intuition

You start to gain momentum only after you take action, but everyone wants the momentum before they start. Keep Newton's First Law of Motion in mind: an object at rest stays at rest and an object in motion stays in motion with the same speed unless acted upon by an external force. An object in motion has momentum, so once you are in motion, you have a natural force keeping you going. Once you start moving toward your BFC, you gain momentum. But you need to set yourself up to win.

It's like going to the gym. You decide the night before to go tomorrow, the morning rolls around, and you are tired and decide to hit snooze. Or you could prepare for success the night before by laying out your workout clothes, so that when you wake up, you put them on, lace up your shoes, and grab your gym bag and water bottle. By getting into action, you won't focus on the feeling of being tired; you will ride the wave of momentum to overcome any reluctance. When you arrive at the gym, you will find yourself empowered to take more action and hit the treadmill.

You begin to walk on the treadmill, which turns into a brisk walk, a jog, and then a full-out sprint. You just needed to start. Notice you did not start with the full-on sprint. You warmed up and built your confidence before you increased your intensity. The smaller actions put you into motion to give you momentum. Most of us go too big too soon, which creates unsustainable change because our minds don't have enough time to process the necessary steps involved.

Our mindsets can move us into action or keep us feeling stuck. Getting unstuck only happens after we have moved into action. Go before you feel ready and see how fast you become. Remember that you are only ever competing against the best version of yourself. As James Clear points out, if you become just 1 percent better each day, you become thirty-seven times better in a year.

We're all familiar with what it means to be in our comfort zones. As we make changes, it's important to stay in that zone at first to develop confidence and build momentum. But within the comfort zone, there is what I like to call the zone of optimal change.

While small steps give us the necessary confidence, we can increase the size of the steps to move toward the edge of our comfort zone. Close to the edge is the zone of optimal change. Like strengthening any muscle in your body, your capacity to make bigger steps will grow over time. To determine the ideal size of the step, we need to ask ourselves two questions:

1. Is it small enough to feel achievable?
2. Is it big enough to feel like movement in the right direction?

If the answer is yes to both, you will experience momentum. If the answer is only yes to one of them, challenge yourself to become curious about what else is possible. You may set a challenge for yourself, reach your goal, and realize you are capable of more. That means you brushed up against your zone of optimal change, and it expands each time you challenge yourself in a new way. This is important to know as you set new goals and make bigger changes in your life. What's most important is that you start. Every time we move toward the change we want to make, we build momentum.

 Hand on Heart

Take a deep breath, and place your hand on your heart and repeat these affirmations until you feel them:

I am worthy of developing new habits that build my momentum. Making change inside my comfort zone will build my confidence to take bigger steps outside my comfort zone.

It's safe to take risks and be vulnerable.

I can trust myself, and celebrating wins helps me build momentum.

What's the next right step for me to take?

P.S. The way to reinforce your newly adopted mindset is to build a habit of success in this new way of being and thinking. Small changes might not be enough to get you where you want to go, but you are building momentum toward bigger steps later.

6
REST, REFLECT, PROTECT

*"Your greatness is limited only by
the investments you make in yourself."*

GRANT CARDONE

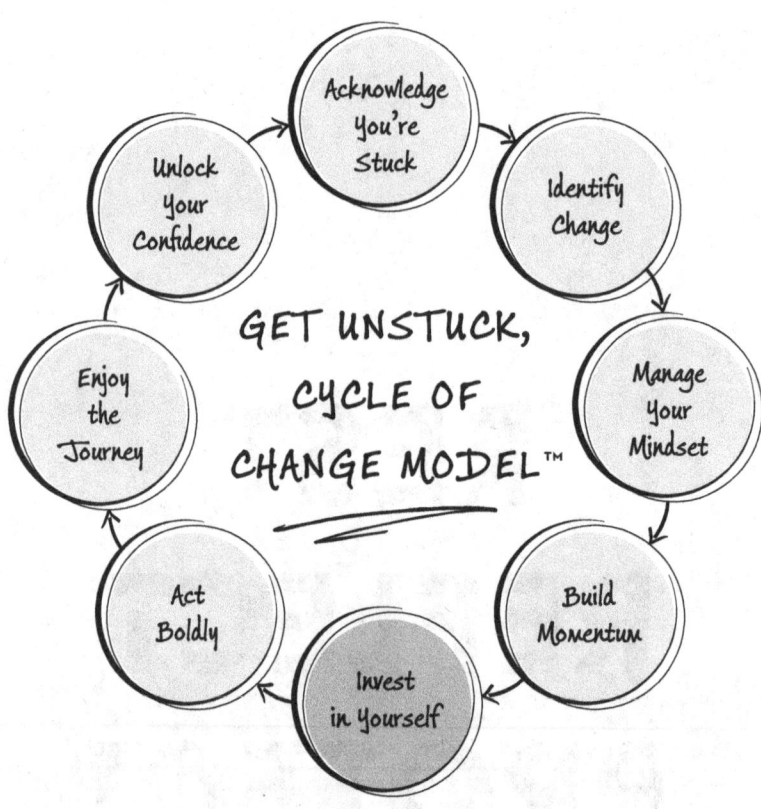

Using the Get Unstuck, Cycle of Change Model, you have realized you are stuck, identified the type of change you want to make, learned to manage your mindset, and built momentum inside your comfort zone. Now it's time to invest in yourself. Pour into yourself like never before, as you develop your confidence along the way.

ANNA WAS A VIBRANT, successful young woman. She had a career as a high-paid corporate accountant, with all the perks that lifestyle afforded: a beach house, sports car, and lots of vacations. When she and her husband, Dan, decided to have a family, they mapped out a plan and agreed that she'd stay home until the kids went to school, and then they'd reevaluate. Anna was ready to give up her career in service of being a stay-at-home mom. It was a good plan. It was sensible. It was culturally acceptable, and it worked for them. Until it didn't.

At first, the sacrifices were fine. Anna didn't mind giving up the daily lattes, lunch meetings, or trendy wardrobe of her favorite heels and classy dresses to go braless, hair pulled into a messy bun, and without makeup. When their first child was born with a breathing condition that required he be hooked up to an oxygen tank, her mothering instinct kicked in at full force. Survival mode became her new normal. Nothing mattered except keeping her son healthy and alive.

She was told her child would never be able to run or become an athlete due to his breathing condition, but that hopefully in time he would breathe on his own. Her hopes and dreams for him were stolen in a moment. After she grieved what she thought motherhood would look like and found acceptance in what actually was, she gained perspective and her compassion for others expanded. We can never understand what people go through, until we go through it ourselves.

Over time, the lack of sleep and self-care, coupled with the constant worry for her son, caused Anna to reach a breaking point. She was exhausted, frequently getting migraines, sleeping poorly, and not connecting with herself, let alone with others. Being so preoccupied with the necessities of taking care of her son and supporting her husband's career, she had forgotten that she was also part of the family. She was the glue holding the family together. She desperately prayed that this period of time would pass and that her son could be like other children, laughing and playing and breathing without an oxygen tank.

She was dedicated to doing everything she could to help her son breathe on his own and did every exercise available. A year passed; their son started getting better and could breathe on his own and even run. Anna began to feel a bit more like herself again and trusted he would be one day an athlete. She was smiling more, felt more peace, and experienced moments of joy. Life was slowly getting better, and she regained some of her energy.

To her delight, she got pregnant with her second child and felt gratitude like never before. She felt excited and hopeful for her growing family, making plans and preparing the baby's room. Life was moving forward.

Five months later, she suffered a painful miscarriage, and her dreams were stripped away from her once again. She questioned why this had happened to her. She was devastated and stuck in trauma from the loss she had experienced. This was one change she could never have been ready to face, let alone accept.

With no emotional resources left, she found herself spiraling into depression, unable to catch her breath or stop her tears; it got worse by the day. She tried to find the joy of motherhood in her heart, but it was constantly overshadowed by fear, grief, and hopelessness.

She had to find her way through the sadness and loss. She called me still in disbelief about what she had just experienced. She could barely talk when we connected.

"I am so lost," she whispered. "I am so stuck in my head. I don't know what to do."

We cried for her lost dreams, for all of the moms who go through miscarriage, infant loss, difficulty conceiving, or pregnancy interruption when a baby is conceived with a rare genetic disease, and for all of the people who experience unexpected grief. It was in that moment that I truly understood the gravity of being stuck. It cost her everything. She was now the one who could hardly breathe.

She was grieving the child she had lost, and more than that too. She lost who she had been before experiencing such a traumatic event. She lost her hope of what she wanted her life to look like—with two healthy children and a white picket fence—and was staring in disbelief at what her life actually was. It was not what she had dreamed of, expected, or wanted. But it was hers to navigate. She needed to change her mindset to change her life.

Desperate to leave her pain in the past, Anna tried to muscle her way through the grief, not realizing that so often with more difficult emotions, the only path forward is to work your way through them. The losses had been piling up around her over the years. The loss of her career. The loss of the little luxuries that she used to enjoy so much, like an afternoon at the spa or lunch with her friends or dates with her husband. The loss of interesting conversations with intellectual peers at work. And biggest of all, the loss of her dream of what her family would be.

She couldn't remember what it felt like to be herself. The sense of peace that used to come so naturally for her had been traded in for heavy sadness, emptiness, and self-judgment that never seemed to leave. She was a prisoner to herself.

When Anna reached out for support, she barely recognized herself or knew who she was, let alone what she needed or how to make change. Like most of us, she had mistakenly believed that her own care was *optional* and that everyone else's needs came first; she felt she could only care for herself once everyone else's needs were satisfied. The problem was that never happened. There was always something else to do, and her needs were pushed off for another day, another week, another month, another time that never arrived. At the end of each night, when her head hit the pillow, she would pray to feel like herself again, but she'd lost hope that it was even possible. She was a shadow of the woman she used to be.

"I am so lost and have no idea how to put myself back together," she shared in our initial coaching session. "I am not sure who I am anymore or what I want to do in my career. Nothing feels right. I don't feel right." Her eyes filled with tears as she looked away.

"I'm sorry," I said, as I touched her shoulder. I took a moment to hold space, sitting with her in this vulnerable time of acknowledging and accepting where she was. Often when we feel lost, it's the result of having lost ourselves one little piece at a time, and then one day, we don't recognize ourselves anymore. It's not only the big things that break us open, but the little cracks that chip away at us. It's the trauma that we push down and don't talk about, it's the relationships that slowly slip away, and it's our hearts that we fail to listen to that causes us to lose ourselves.

What happened to Anna happens to many of us. We make changes in our lives believing they are for a season of life, and we make sacrifices we deem necessary—and sometimes they are. We do what we think we should do, and we forget to take care of ourselves along the way. We lose our energy, we fail to rest, and we lack boundaries. At some level, whether we recognize it or not, we feel guilty if we take time for ourselves, so we fail to rest again. We ignore the need to check in with ourselves and reflect, and we forget to protect our energy, unaware of all the things that add up and drain us. We fall apart one piece at a time and eventually become a shadow of the person we used to be. Our needs, feelings, and experiences are important because they have shaped us into the person we are—and being in tune with them will take us to who we will become.

Resting, reflecting, and protecting our energy are the ways to save ourselves on the darkest days and amid the greatest challenges. Not being true to ourselves, our own needs, or our own desires can lead to regret. We regret what we did not do, what we did do, and what we should have done better. Regret gets us nowhere fast.

The Truth about Regret

Bronnie Ware, a palliative care provider, said that among the greatest regrets people have as they die is "I wish I'd had the courage to live a life true to myself, not the life others expected of me." *Psychology*

Today explains, "Stringently adhering to cultural norms at the expense of your own passions will result in disappointment and bitterness." Taking care of our needs is our greatest responsibility and the best way to prevent us from having regret. But it's never that easy, is it?

We are all programmed to try to do what is right, to follow expectations and norms. Sometimes, that comes at a significant cost; we lose ourselves along the way as we fail to be true to our own self. We stop listening to ourselves and trusting our own intuition. It may seem insignificant in the moment, but over time we compromise who we are, which has a significant cost—our peace. Anna did what she thought she should by becoming a stay-at-home mom to start a family. Looking back, she realized she gave up on her career and then herself during that season. Her new reality of struggle, stress, and loss took over her identity.

She knew she could rebuild her career, but she was unsure if she could rebuild herself. In the process of neglecting her needs, she lost her ability to trust herself. Anna was waiting for things to change before she could make a change. She wanted to have all her ducks in a row before she took action. But in waiting, time was flying by.

We tend to focus externally rather than look inside to make change. We wait for permission from others before we move forward, and when we are lost, change becomes that much more out of reach. It doesn't have to be this way. As women, we have multiple roles and responsibilities. We hustle hard to meet demands, often neglecting to take care of ourselves along the way. We stay busy fulfilling other people's demands on our time and feel guilty about reclaiming that time for ourselves. We end up feeling unfulfilled and unable to sit with ourselves comfortably; we chase the next opportunity hoping for a gratifying moment or distraction that keeps our minds and hearts from accepting that we need to make a change. We try to keep the peace in all aspects of our relationships, unaware that in doing so we lose our peace within, which is at the greatest cost to ourselves and our soul.

It seems easier to wait for circumstance and opportunity to align before we decide to take action. It's harder to look inside and discover what is really holding us back and to address our fear. Resting is the first step of investing in ourselves before we make significant change. If you want to make a BFC, there will be fear. You will want to wait to feel ready and look externally for things to align before making change.

There is a better way though. When we choose to invest in ourselves, we stop waiting for circumstances or other people to change; we look inside ourselves to make the change. We find courage and strength to make change. We trust ourselves because we know ourselves.

The process of truly investing in ourselves includes resting to slow down and recharge, reflecting to check in with ourselves for clarity, and protecting our boundaries so that we can manage and maintain our energetic levels. This is especially hard to do when we feel we need to make urgent change. When we consider how much energy is required to meet the demands made on us, rest is important. When we rest, reflect, and protect, we can show up as our most authentic selves and embrace change with less resistance and more ease.

Resting Is Investing

Resting is often not on the top of our priority list, yet rest gives us clarity to move forward. We often feel guilty taking time to rest, especially when we have lots to accomplish in a day. We have the mentality to push through and keep going, even when we are drained. The truth is rest is productive. It allows us to build up our resources and energy. In *Rest*, author Alex Soojung-Kim Pang suggests we work fewer hours but more intensely, because shorter time periods increase productivity; the ideal number of hours of work is four per day. He advises deliberately resting at least as much as you work, as well as deepening our time for play with challenging, engaging activities.

Pang explains, "The 'resting' brain turns out to be consolidating memories, making sense of the past, and searching for solutions to problems that are occupying our waking hours." Resting is a necessity for all of us, and we need it to evolve into the next version of ourselves and to find solutions to our problems. Yet rest is often neglected.

When life is demanding, it is hard to find time to rest. I get it. Anna was so stuck in her grief that she didn't know how she could feel better. She was always pressed on time as the demands on her continued to increase. She didn't think taking care of herself would ever happen. We discussed that even when she was busy, she needed to learn to give herself some space to rest and that it was okay; that any little bit of time was better than no time at all. For those of us who are type A or go-all-in people, it's hard to accept that we should do anything just a little. But a little is better than none, and done is better than perfect.

Anna had to start small and learn how to physically rest and how to mentally and emotionally enjoy rest with a two-year-old at home. She started by learning to take deep breaths. She intentionally took long breaths to slow down her nervous system, sitting in a chair and breathing deeply for a minute at a time. She had never given her breath much attention before, and she now noticed that her breath tended to be quite shallow.

How is your breathing? Do you slow down to take deep breaths? I encourage you to try it now. Deep breathing calms your nervous system and allows you to be more productive. Take a few long deep breaths in and out, and see how you feel.

Anna also started sitting down to drink water throughout the day to give her moments of rest, when she didn't have minutes of rest. This is how she started to make time to rest. A few other behaviors slowly started to come together, combining to form the beginning of her routine of self-care, self-love, and rest.

She learned that when she took a hot bath at night, she slept better, and when she slept better, she felt better. She started spending a few minutes in the morning reading an article that stimulated her mind, as she loved to be challenged intellectually. These small behaviors gave her pockets of rest that fueled her days and helped her start feeling more like herself again.

After a few months of taking moments and minutes for herself, she started baking again, something she loved but had stopped doing. She started painting again, which sparked her creative side. She needed to get out of her rut of only cooking, cleaning, and taking care of her child every minute of every day. Joyful and fulfilling activities gave her the rest she needed and refueled her. It's not all about sitting down and physically resting. Doing new activities can allow us to rest as well.

So often, all-or-nothing thinking takes over: we believe that if we can't do a lot of something, it's not worth doing it at all. Every minute you spend on yourself for yourself adds up and is worth it because you are worth it. Learning how to be more and do less is valuable for all of us, at any stage of life.

Anna so desperately wanted to get back to her old identity of being a successful corporate accountant, but there was a big gap to cross from where she was currently standing. It had only been two years since she worked in the corporate world, so it was not the gap in terms of time, but the gap in her identity and soul. She was different now, changed forever. She knew her work made her feel alive and stimulated her, and she craved intellectual conversations. But she was unsure how she could be a good mom and an ambitious career woman. She couldn't see what her next step was until she gave herself permission to rest. She was stuck on a hamster wheel of hustling, afraid that if she stepped off, she would lose her groove and never be able to get back on.

Over the next few months, she started carving out little pockets of time to invest in herself. Her rest included going for walks by herself and singing along to her favorite music. Instead of listening to podcasts and being productive all the time, she gave herself permission just to be. When she returned home from her walks, she would journal, asking herself these two questions: "How am I doing?" and "What do I need?" New answers came to her each time she took the time to rest and reflect.

Research shows that using a different part of the brain can be considered a form of rest. Pang notes that studies by neuroscientists suggest that our resting brain is still active: "The brain automatically switches on a default mode network . . . a series of interconnected sections that activate as soon as people stop concentrating on external tasks, and shifts from outward-focused to inward-focused cognition." When we no longer focus on *doing* specific tasks (like reading,

As women, we have multiple roles and responsibilities. We hustle hard to meet demands, often neglecting to take care of ourselves along the way.

working, or writing) and take a moment to focus inward, we activate different parts of our brain. The same is true when we let our minds wander as we stare out the window. Even when we are not focused on doing anything, our brain is still on. Our brain is *always* active, even when we think we are not doing anything. Allowing your brain to move between different modes is a form of rest. In fact, it is productive to do so, so don't feel guilty when you take some time to invest in yourself and rest.

The most important point is to rest by doing an activity that is not typical for you. For someone in research, resting may be climbing a mountain; for an athlete, rest may be meditation or hot and cool baths. Rest is switching from our automatic mode of functioning to another way of being. Rest is not only necessary, but it increases your productivity and will lead you to the clarity that you crave. Resting gives you more energy. But first, you need to give yourself permission to slow down.

Slow Down to Speed Up

Sometimes in life you just need to slow down. Working harder and longer often does not get us the results we crave. We are taught to think reward follows work, but if our work is never done, we don't reach the rewards. Slowing down and taking time to rest, reflect, and protect your energy will help you speed up later and achieve your big goals.

You can do a million things in a day that are not aligned with your vision, or your values, but if you do one thing that is totally aligned, it can set a million opportunities into motion, like dominos put into motion with one single gentle tap. There is something inside you that you are meant to do, and that is aligned with your highest self and congruent with the desires of your soul. Your BFC will come to you when you slow down.

When we rush to get everything done, we often miss that one aligned and powerful thing, which means the chain of change—the dominos—stay upright. If we slow down, we are more likely to zero in on our first domino, which means we will make faster progress later.

Slowing down also moves you from your sympathetic nervous system response (fight or flight) into your parasympathetic nervous system response (rest and digest). Your parasympathetic nervous system is designed to conserve energy. Your sympathetic nervous system carries signals that put your body's systems on alert to keep you safe. If we are operating for long periods of time with our sympathetic nervous system as our default setting, we find it very challenging to slow down. Because our nervous system does not calm down, we struggle to give ourselves space to rest and be.

Your parasympathetic system signals relaxation and allows you to feel calm. Slowing down is good for your nervous system and good for you. Slowing down gives your sympathetic nervous system a break and brings you clarity. Sometimes without awareness, we choose to stay busy because it distracts us and helps us avoid what we know we need to do or face. It's as if we are playing a game with ourselves. If we stay busy, we won't have to deal with that thing. Truth is, if you avoid it and stay busy, that thing will deal with you. It always does. It never goes away. Slowing down often brings up the things you have been trying to avoid. This is a gift though. It's your soul speaking to you and telling you what's necessary.

It's healthy to slow down and give yourself rest. Here are some helpful ways to activate your parasympathetic nervous system:

1. **Deep Breathing:** You can try the box method of four counts in, hold for four counts, out for four counts, and hold for four counts. Imagine you are breathing in the shape of a box.

2. **EFT Tapping:** Emotional freedom technique can be a quick and powerful way to slow racing thoughts and connect with your body. Name your emotions and affirm yourself positively while tapping your body's chakras. You can state the feeling you are experiencing and reinforce yourself by saying, "I deeply love and respect myself. Even though I don't feel ready to go after my BFC, I deeply love and respect myself."

3. **Gratitude and Appreciation:** Reflecting on what you are grateful for calms your nervous system. When you send a message to someone

showing your appreciation, you activate a part of your brain that calms your nervous system. Research about gratitude has shown that the hippocampus and amygdala—two regions of your brain in charge of regulating emotions, memory, and bodily functioning—get activated with feelings of gratitude. Studies also show that gratitude releases toxic emotions, reduces pain, improves quality of sleep, aids in stress reduction, and reduces levels of anxiety and depression.

4. **Listening to Music or Dancing:** Music calms and soothes your mind, body, and soul. Adding in movement allows you to connect back with your body and to release stress.

5. **Eating and Drinking:** The quickest way to switch into our parasympathetic nervous system is to eat or drink something. Remember to make a healthy choice when you do this, like a cup of tea or a piece of fruit.

We know that eating healthily, sleeping well, and exercising are ways to take care of ourselves. Investing in yourself means taking time to rest, reflect, and protect. Investing in yourself means different things to different people. In its simplest form, it means time to slow down and rest with reflection and intention so that you can experience connection with yourself. Connecting to yourself is essential to your well-being. Connecting with your innermost thoughts and feelings provides you with greater clarity on how to move forward, especially when you are at a crossroads and want to make a BFC.

Just so we are clear, I am not talking about the bare minimum of self-care, like taking a shower and making sure to eat on days we are pressed for time. Meeting basic human needs is just that: a necessity that every human needs to survive.

Most people live day-to-day, getting by, and just surviving. I don't want that for you. You can make your BFC by using the Get Unstuck, Cycle of Change Model so you navigate your path forward with confidence. The best way to discover your greatness is to invest in yourself and take time to ask yourself some intentional questions. Living by design is more powerful and purposeful than living by default. Operating on autopilot, going through the motions, and not paying attention to your needs and desires is hardly making the most out of life. When you rest and reflect, you gain clarity and wisdom that will help you take the next right step. Here are some simple ways to do this:

- Slow down and check in with yourself—including with your breath.
- Ask yourself what you need and how you are doing.
- Think about what brings you joy.
- Do an activity that brings you joy.
- Reflect on all that is going right in your life.
- Protect yourself by making decisions that support your boundaries.

Think about the people and responsibilities in your life that give you energy and those that take your energy. Try to increase the people and activities that give you energy and decrease the ones that drain your energy.

You deserve to feel your best and have your needs met, especially when you are approaching a BFC. It's important to feel loved, worthy, and empowered to live more bravely and feel more alive so you can start to thrive. Pouring into yourself first will help you make the change you truly desire. Loving yourself so much that you radiate love, joy, and energy attracts the right opportunities and people to your life. I promise the best investment you can make is in yourself—always. It always comes back to you.

Now, the real point of rest is to make space for possibility. In this phase, you plant the seed of possibility. You create space so that you can see opportunity, solutions, and abundance. You give your brain permission to dream, and you let solutions come to you rather than try to control every outcome. It's about relieving pressure so you can allow something new in. Simply put, when you are not well rested, your nervous system has less capacity to handle change. Your brain can get stuck in defense mode, trying to keep you safe. Resting builds up your reserves and gives you access to the courage to make change. As a bonus, resting calms your nervous system, moving from sympathetic to parasympathetic. Sometimes you don't realize how stressed, how lost, or how tired you are until you feel your nervous system relax.

If you take time to rest and recharge your batteries, you won't operate on empty. You will move through life with more grace and energy because you have a reserve of energy. You will vibrate at a higher energetic level and attract more of what is meant for you with ease. When we take a moment to reflect, isn't that what we all want? More ease, less stress. More traction, less friction. This is all available to you when you slow down to rest.

Reflection Is the Missing Link

Maybe you are thinking that you already take time for self-care. You do all the things people recommend, like going for a massage, getting your nails done, or hitting the gym. These are all great things to do, but to move into action to make a BFC, the key is to combine rest with reflection. If you have been taking holidays, carving out time for meditation, watching your favorite TV show, or reading a book and still feel a bit low on energy, try to add the reflection component and see how your mind expands as you open to possibility.

It's powerful to be aware of how you feel—notice if you are feeling tired, energized, or sad in your current state. Some helpful questions to reflect on are here for you to explore:

- How am I doing today?
- What do I need today?
- What would bring me joy?
- How am I serving myself?
- How am I serving others today?
- How can I put better boundaries in place to reach my goals?
- What changes do I need to make to support the BFC I want to make in my life?

Rest is not solely about recharging when we feel tired; it's an intentional practice that includes reflection. Reflection helps you connect with yourself. Sometimes when we are tired, we think we just need more sleep. But there are two types of tired: one that requires resting your physical body so that you gain back your energy, and one that requires internal mindful rest which provides peace of mind and the peace within your soul.

I like to think of peace as a deep knowing, an understanding of who we are, where we are going, and why we are moving in that direction with alignment and purpose. I think internal peace gives us the most rest long term and fuels our body with energy. Peace is not about the absence of conflict or challenges; it's about the ability to have space between what is happening and how we are feeling. It is the ability to have freedom to be yourself and experience a state of calmness within. Peace opens you up to possibility in the best kind of way as your energy changes. People notice your energetic state and want to be around you. Peace brings forward possibilities and attracts opportunities and people to you. You get to work less hard and receive greater opportunities, which is an incredible return on investment.

When you contemplate your BFC, you lack peace of mind because no decision is perfect. You waffle because you have not been there before exploring new territory. You are in a storm of emotions because you are desperate to get out of your current state, but you don't know how. I get it. I have been there many times, and continue to get caught in the storm, but it does get easier when you learn the Get Unstuck, Cycle of Change Model and make yourself a priority while experiencing changes.

No BFC is easy. I wish I could tell you it is. There is always risk to making a BFC, but when you know who you are and your vision for your life, you can handle the bumps and bruises easier. Two things can be true at once: making a choice to move in one direction can be positive and hard. Right and challenging. Rewarding and scary. Every decision has its pros and cons. When we truly know what is important to us, we can make the most favorable choice long term. A decision can be bittersweet and still be the right decision. It's okay to grieve your old identity you are letting go of as you make space for

**More ease, less stress.
More traction, less friction.**
This is all available
to you when you
slow down to rest.

your new identity you are stepping into. BFCs do this, and it's good for you. You've got to let go of the old to let in the new.

In preparation for a BFC, reflection gives you an accurate picture of what is going on so you can move forward with insight. When we rest, we have time to reflect and take an inventory of our resources including demands on our day, energy levels, and mental clarity. When we focus on our internal resources available, they can fuel us long term and we can take care of ourselves along the way.

Consider these questions:

- What do I need to say no to today so I can say yes to myself?
- What resources do I have to support me as I step toward change?
- What aspects of my life lack support?
- How can I acquire additional support where needed?
- How am I feeling today?
- What is on my heart today?
- How can I take care of myself better?
- What will bring me joy today?

Investing in yourself allows you to discover and reconnect with your values, beliefs, and motivations, and in doing so, you learn to trust yourself and ask for what you need. You discover that you can communicate what you need and expect, and that it's safe to do so. You become active in your own life and start designing your life to work for you, with you, and through you. Becoming who we are meant to be and living life to the fullest is what we all want, don't we?

Investing in yourself is the one item on your endless to-do list that will give you momentum like nothing else. But the catch-22 is that you have to put yourself on the list, make yourself a priority, and then follow through. Knowing who you are, where you are going, and what you want will give you clarity about the steps you are about to take with precision. You begin to operate with ease and flow at a faster pace because you have done the necessary inner work. Your soul has a place to rest in and your body has a soul to navigate from. Resting is investing. You are worthy of rest, sister.

Your Energy Is Your Highest Currency

Resting and reflecting pays other dividends. Have you ever noticed when someone magnetic walks into the room? You can't help but notice them—their style, grace, and energy. You feel different around them; you relax and your breathing slows down. You tell them things you would never tell a stranger. After you meet them, you find yourself saying, "Wow, that person has such great energy." They are connected with themselves, and often something larger than themselves, so they can show up fully in life and connect with others. They are safe and comfortable in who they are. Their presence is welcoming and encourages you to feel comfortable being who you are too. They are present, fully expressed, and invite others to do the same just by their essence.

If you have not experienced meeting a magnetic person like this, chances are you have noticed the opposite and remember being around someone with negative energy that brought you down without them even saying a word. You could just feel it. What you feel impacts your energetic and vibrational levels. Trust me when I say that your energy matters and either opens up doors of possibility or slams doors in your face.

We never fully understand the opportunity cost of spending time with people who have the wrong kind of energy. It may seem like no big deal at the time, but think about all the possibilities for your life. Realize that every decision you make always has an impact, positive or negative, instant or delayed, expansive or contractive. Being aligned with people and opportunities gives you energy, and you will feel good around them. I have been invited to speak at events simply based on my energy. I recently got asked by bestselling author and entrepreneur Mike Michalowicz to speak at his conference after a lunch with mutual friends. He said he liked my energy. Energy speaks volumes as people can feel it.

As we learned in chapter 3, roughly 95 percent of our decisions are emotionally based. Those decisions could be about what to eat, when to go to bed, who we spend time with, what to purchase, and what we do each day. Paying attention to your feelings taps into your intuition, which can save you time as well as mental, physical, and emotional energy. However, the challenge is that most of us suppress our emotions and try to act logically. We are also so busy doing things, we forget to tap into our feelings. Neuroscientist Antonio Damasio has called humans "feeling machines that think" and suggests our instinct for feelings is more refined and developed than our ability to think.

Protect Your Energy and Your Resources

By taking care of ourselves and putting ourselves on our own to-do list, we prioritize ourselves. We also need to become protective of our resources: our time, energy, money, and capacity to be in relationships. Protecting our energetic resources is a necessary part of taking care of ourselves. Boundaries are positive and necessary for all of us if we want to step into the fullest expression of ourselves. Boundaries are beautiful. They keep us safe. They inform others of our needs and keep us in our optimal energetic state. Boundaries also provide us with a place to experience self-love and self-acceptance and become truly comfortable with who we are and where we are going.

We are meant to change and evolve. It's a good thing. Give yourself permission to change your mind and adjust as you pay attention to your needs. We can't be all things to all people, but we certainly can be *more* for ourselves. Boundaries mean that you understand your needs and values and what's important to you, and that you protect and honor yourself. This is especially important when we are leveling up. When you are stepping into the next version of yourself, your needs, priorities, and preferences will change. It's your responsibility to teach people how to treat you and to take care of yourself in the process.

Terri Cole is a licensed psychotherapist and leading expert in mindfulness, meditation, relationships, and well-being. In her book *Boundary Boss*, she explains, "Healthy boundaries are generous *and* efficient. When they're in place, you will be amazed at how much time, energy, and bandwidth you have." Cole writes, "Personal boundaries are like a guidebook that you create to clearly identify permissible ways that other people may behave toward you."

If you understand the importance of self-care and you spend time reflecting on your needs, but you do not protect your energy, you will always feel depleted. Change will feel challenging because you are drained and lack the necessary bandwidth to take the next right step. All three elements are necessary: slowing down to rest, checking in with yourself to reflect, and protecting your energy with boundaries.

Boundaries help you maintain your heart's greatest desires and transition from thinking to doing, to becoming, to being. Boundaries can feel uncomfortable at first because we lack experience with them. Let's think about a conflict we are currently experiencing and reflect on the boundaries that would be helpful to have based on your needs, preferences, and desires. Think of three boundaries that would be helpful for you to have. Write them down.

My client Anna gave up her career to raise a family, and she admitted she stopped paying attention to her boundaries. She didn't know what was draining her energy, but it was always drained. She was in a constant state of exhaustion. Can you relate to this? I know I sure can. She tried to keep up with her social obligations, family commitments, and friendly neighborhood chat, which depleted her already drained battery. She functioned on autopilot, going through the motions.

When she was preparing to go back to her corporate accounting career, I asked her what gave her energy and what drained her energy. At first, she had no clue because she'd never thought about this before. Most of us go through the motions without intention, never reflecting on our energy levels.

When she returned to work, she paid attention to her energy levels and noticed that commuting downtown each day was hard. It was a long ride, and she hated traffic. She noticed that one of her coworkers, Micah, always greeted her with a big smile and gave her energy, making her feel positive. Anna also noticed another coworker, Kelly, sucked her energy; she didn't enjoy her job and always focused on the negative. Simply noticing how she felt in other people's presence allowed Anna to start making better decisions that served her. She learned that it was her job to protect her energy, and she needed some boundaries to do so. Awareness is always the first step to making change.

Some things we cannot remove altogether, but we can certainly shift. Anna limited her time with Energy-Killer Kelly, started listening to podcasts and her favorite playlists on her drive (rather than the radio with ads that annoyed her), and tried to have a conversation with Marvelous Micah when she arrived at work to begin her day in a positive mood. Anna became intentional with her energy.

Anna also struggled with telling her boss she needed to leave at 4:30 p.m. to pick up her son from daycare. She felt guilty that she couldn't work late. But then she realized that leaving at 4:30 p.m. was the right thing for her family and it was okay to ask. This was a boundary she needed to set because her life was different now. She was a mother, and the expectation needed to change. After avoiding having the conversation, she finally mustered up enough courage and asked her boss about leaving at 4:30 p.m. To her surprise, he agreed right away. She felt lighter and learned that putting boundaries in place is positive and beneficial.

After about a year, Anna started feeling better in her life and was making herself a priority every day, even if it was for a ten-minute workout to her favorite songs, journaling to check in with herself, slowing down to eat her meals, or spending time soaking in the bath at night. She knew it was hard to get a solid hour at any time, so instead she found blocks of ten minutes just for herself, and she was intentional about that time. She would remind herself that she was investing in herself. This made her feel good about her decision rather than guilty about it. She understood that if she did not care for her needs first, she would run out of resources for the people and projects she cared about.

Sometimes avoiding doing or saying what is needed taps our energy and has a cost. It mentally consumes, physically drains, and emotionally occupies us. Not making the change we want also has a cost. When we postpone the inevitable, we delay what is really meant for us and who we are meant to become. What is it that you know you need to do to protect your boundaries and your energy?

Hand on Heart

Affirm yourself with these words:

I am worthy of my desires. Investing in myself is the best investment I can make. Resting with reflection will give me the clarity and confidence to move forward. It is safe to rest, reflect, and protect my energy. I am worthy to rest as I am. I am safe to rest. I deserve to rest.

Take a few deep breaths, place your hand on your heart, and check in with yourself.

How am I feeling?
What do I need?
How can I take better care of myself today?
What boundaries do I need to put into place?
What gives me energy?
What drains my energy?
Who gives me energy?
Who takes my energy?

P.S. Building capacity in your life opens you to the possibility of bigger change. You will still experience fear, and that's a normal part of the process. It's time to dance with fear.

7
ACT BOLDLY

*"All growth starts at
the end of your comfort zone."*

TONY ROBBINS

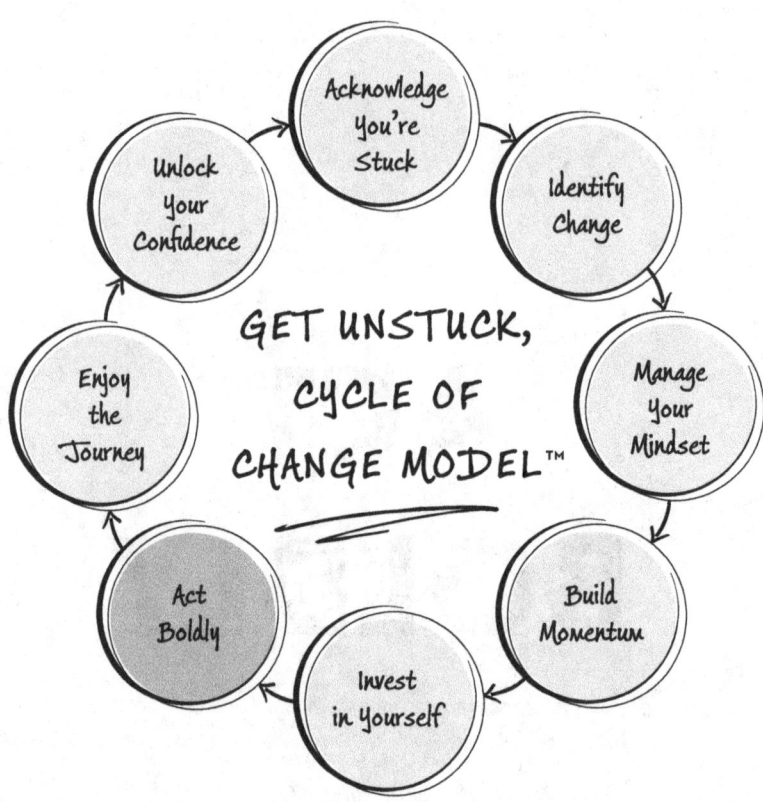

After acknowledging you're stuck, identifying your BFC, managing your mindset, building momentum, and investing in yourself, it's time to act boldly. And that means moving outside your comfort zone. You will embrace your fear and take it with you as you take action.

GENEVIEVE WAS a faithful wife and a loving mother to her two boys. She was devoted to building a remarkable life for her husband and children. She spent twenty years putting everything she had into making that possible. She was the kind of woman that others look at and say, "How do you do it all?" She was a stay-at-home mom and always made time for one-on-ones with her kids, tirelessly took on most of the domestic responsibilities, and planned monthly dates with her husband to keep the spark alive. And yet she couldn't even remember what the spark felt like anymore or why she was trying so hard.

Even though everything looked fine on paper, Genevieve felt as though she was being slowly crushed under a growing weight of disappointment in her marriage, each day a little heavier than the day before. She was living comfortably in misery. She hung on to hope and believed that if she only tried harder or did things differently, her marriage could work. No matter what she did or how hard she tried, her husband was always ready with a sharp criticism in hand—about her looks, her character, her work, and even her parenting. Nothing seemed good enough. She always felt like she was too much, not enough, and never just right. She desperately prayed for courage, for strength to move outside her comfort zone, and for bravery to do what she had been avoiding for years. She was stuck in fear, unable to take any action.

To others, Genevieve was a loving friend, a devoted mother, a stylish and beautiful woman, a leader in her church, and someone to emulate. She was kind and generous. She seemed to radiate pure joy. But to her husband, she was one disappointment after another. He said she was always nagging him and that he always felt pressure when he was around her. All she desired was a connection with him and to share her deepest desires with him. She thought that by being honest and expressing her needs and desires, she could have a healthy marriage in which they could both thrive. The more she shared, the more he withdrew.

She was brought up to work hard, appreciate what you had, look for the good in others, and never give up, so that's what she had been doing. But the thought of another decade of that same marital dynamic crushed her soul and felt unbearable. The weight she was carrying was heavy and she could no longer pretend, cover it up, or hide from it. She was becoming it.

The heaviness of that relationship found its way into many other areas of Genevieve's life. She became insecure and anxious, questioning her abilities that she used to feel confident about. Her mind was always racing, and she was walking on eggshells, wondering how her husband would react. Anxiety set in, and she no longer had the mental strength to keep pushing through. In all of the tiptoeing, she lost her stride. As she constantly tried to improve herself, to be seen as good, beautiful, and worthy of love and appreciation, she lost hope. She was already a people pleaser, wanting to do the right thing, and his avoidant behavior planted new insecurities. Their communication became nonexistent, and they tried to tolerate each other for the sake of the children. He never told her she was beautiful, he seldom thanked her for anything, and he rarely even bothered to ask how she was doing. They became strangers living under the same roof.

Like many women, Genevieve thought it was her fault, that she had to earn love and be better at striving for perfection. She loved him and wanted her marriage to work out more than he could ever imagine, but the toll on her mental wellness was becoming unbearable. Her body followed suit with weariness and exhaustion. She couldn't find the energy that had once been her trademark. The spark in her eyes faded and the joy she once had was now a distant memory.

In a conversation with her, Genevieve told me, "I'm starting to think it's not about working harder anymore, and it's out of my control. I have tried everything and hung on to hope, and now my hope is gone too. It's just that we just don't *fit* anymore. It's like I am trying to fit a square peg in a round hole, and I can't keep trying. I don't think he even likes me anymore." Tears rolled down her cheeks. "I'm so exhausted trying to make things work."

It had been clear to her for quite some time that she needed to leave her marriage to save herself, a seemingly impossible situation to be faced with, especially because she had two boys she adored. She had thought she would suck it up in favor of supporting the family but failed to acknowledge she was part of the family, the glue holding it together. She was physically there but emotionally distracted. She did everything for everyone, and it was no longer a healthy environment for her. It had become clear to her that the only way out from under the weight of her pain was to get out of her marriage and embrace the fear. This was her invitation to act boldly and step out of her comfort zone.

For someone like Genevieve, that was no easy decision. She wasn't sure that she could do it. She'd contemplated and waffled for ten years. She desperately wanted to be a good and faithful wife and mother. If she could try harder, suppress her feelings more, not make a big deal out of things, then maybe, just maybe, it could work. In her long process of trying, she had failed to understand she was abandoning herself in hopes of saving her marriage. She believed that marriage vows were the most sacred, never to be broken, a belief that was shared by her community, closest friends, and family. What would *they* say if she left her husband? Would she be trading the judgment of her husband for the judgment of her community? Or would this one pivotal decision bring her back to a place of self-acceptance where she could find her joy again? She wondered if she would be better off in an empty marriage than in no marriage at all.

She worried about her now-grown children. How would they take it? Would they feel betrayed by her and think it was all her fault? Would they be hurt in the process? Would she lose her relationship with either or *both* of them? Or would they understand and support her over time and be grateful for her courage to do what was hard but necessary?

Genevieve's financial situation was also a serious concern because a divorce would decimate her finances. She would most certainly lose her beloved home that she took so much pride in. She felt guilty about asking her husband for much spousal support, as she was the one who stayed at home to raise the children. She gave everything to her family and would leave with nothing.

It was clear to Genevieve that if she left her marriage, *everything* she knew would be changed forever and she would have to create a new life from scratch. At fifty years old, would she be better off to stay or better off to go? With her children now off to university, she felt like it was finally her time to make herself a priority.

So many aspects of Genevieve's identity overlapped with her firm commitment to the sacred vow of marriage that it was hard for her to imagine who she would even be—who she *could* be—if she walked away from it. Genevieve strove to be faithful and honest in everything that she did. Would she be those things if she left her marriage? No one in her entire extended family was divorced, and it would be a new label she would have to wear. Her identity was so wrapped up in who she was in relation to others, she forgot who she was to herself. If she was not a faithful, hardworking wife, then who was she? All parts of her were changing, and every signal was indicating to her that she had to act boldly. She finally gave herself permission to make the change that she needed by ending her marriage to save herself; she had entered the Get Unstuck, Cycle of Change Model.

When it comes to consequential decisions, we rarely feel an abundance of confidence. Genevieve was no different.

"No matter how much I plan and prepare, once I leave my marriage, I will be different *forever*," she told me between sobs. "Will I lose everything in pursuit of finding myself again?"

I held her hand. "Everything will feel different, and that's okay. What's not okay is to live in constant turmoil, pain, stress, anxiety, and disappointment. There is a significant cost to that. The cost of putting your life on hold. You can only change yourself and make change *for* yourself. It's okay to let go." I held back tears, knowing how hard she had tried and how desperately she wanted her marriage to work.

It seemed as if the moment she acknowledged her fears out loud, Genevieve started to accept the possibility of a new reality and identity, and she even found some power in the midst of her pain. Facing her fear gave her a glimpse into possibility. She was scared, sad, angry, disappointed, and grieving. In all her efforts to keep the peace with her partner, she had started a war inside herself.

In the process of losing ourselves or stepping into a new version of ourselves, we feel lost and fearful. Acting boldly requires us to step outside our comfort zone, ready or not, and move through fear. Often the only way to make the hard decision is to decide and then act boldly. The only way to prepare is to surrender to what is, even when it sucks. Sometimes the only way to make progress is to walk away. The only way to heal a broken heart is to break it fully open. It happens to all of us, whatever *it* is we need to let go of, however hard or long we held on. Change is hard, and grieving is a necessary part of the process.

We grieve our old identities, wishes, and hopes in addition to what was lost. What's beautiful is that we can create something new in time. Something that is aligned. Something that fits. Something that lasts, with less pain and more pleasure. Less stress and more joy. Less trying and more enjoying. Less friction and more flow. Less bending and more becoming.

A new identity often cannot be formed until we have fully let go of the old identity that we held for so long. Feeling lost is part of the process. If we try to create change with our old mindset and way of thinking, we are using part of our identity that needs to be updated. We experience transformation when we fully let go. It's in the messy middle part, the in-between process of letting go and recreating ourselves, that we discover the next version of ourselves waiting for us.

Genevieve had always been praised for being loyal and hardworking, and she didn't want to abandon those qualities. Yet she also realized that although those qualities were true about her, they were also limiting her because of the weight she placed on them to define who she was. She had thought that being loyal meant staying in her marriage at all costs, even if those were abandoning herself and her peace. She thought working hard meant she could never give up.

She now understood that even as a divorced woman, she could still be hardworking and loyal. When she kept integrity with herself, her defining qualities would remain. Her relationship to another person could change, but she would still have these qualities within. This was an empowering moment for her. She was more than that. She wouldn't let her external circumstance define who she was internally. She hadn't been able to put her finger on what exactly had been keeping her from taking action no matter how much she prayed for a sign. It turned out it was herself, her perception of herself, and her fear of creating a new identity. So often, we can stand in our own way without even realizing it, unaware of the true obstacles. Fear clouds our judgment, and only when we are willing to let go do we see things clearly and the sun starts to shine again. Her divorce wouldn't define her. She would be a woman who went through a divorce and not define herself as a divorced woman. She would define herself as a woman of integrity.

This was her time to act boldly, step outside her comfort zone into the unknown of uncertainty, and enter into the zone of possibility. When she stepped away from her reality, she allowed the next version of herself to emerge. As she closed the door behind her, she left the woman she was and met the woman she would soon become.

"I am so overwhelmed. I don't know what to do after I leave," she said.

"How do you want to feel after you leave?" I asked.

"I want to feel like myself again," she whispered.

"Of course you do. You might even become a better version of yourself."

She tried to force a smile with tears running down her cheeks. "This is so scary and overwhelming." It was clear she could not even imagine that her life could get better.

"You will be okay," I assured her.

To help her navigate the change she was stepping into, I asked her to think about how she could prepare mentally, physically, and emotionally for this significant change, with the intention to reveal the steps she would take.

Focusing on how change impacts us mentally, physically, and emotionally is helpful when approaching a BFC that impacts our identity. Painting the picture of how we will evolve through change and the necessary action steps along the way helps us to embrace our fear, keep our word to ourselves, and navigate the Get Unstuck, Cycle of Change Model. As a result, we can evolve into the best version of ourselves.

Stepping Outside Your Comfort Zone

Now let me be clear, acting boldly does not need to be as big and significant as Genevieve's choice to leave a significant relationship. Acting boldly is about stepping outside your comfort zone and embracing fear in pursuit of being true to yourself. It's choosing yourself and what's right for you, doing things differently to get different results. Genevieve made small changes inside her comfort zone until there was nowhere else to move except outside her comfort zone for change to occur. Acting boldly is about making a decision that requires courage, not confidence. Remember that you develop confidence through taking action, not before.

Acting boldly could be as simple as speaking up when your coffee order is wrong instead of remaining silent as you usually do to avoid making a fuss. Acting boldly could be having a hard but necessary conversation that you have been avoiding at work. Acting boldly could be putting better boundaries in place and saying no to obligations and invitations that no longer serve you. Acting boldly is doing things differently and learning to trust yourself in the process as you honor your needs, values, and vision.

When you want different results in your life, you need to make bolder decisions that bring you beyond your normal. Acting boldly is about going against your usual tendencies and respecting and honoring your own needs and desires. Acting boldly involves putting boundaries in place to protect yourself and your inner peace. Acting boldly requires you to act in integrity and in alignment with yourself, no matter the discomfort. It's bold to be true to yourself.

Why We Resist Identity Change

Let's be real. We are all creatures of habit. Genevieve is not alone. Most people avoid uncertainty and change at all costs, especially when the stakes are high and we are afraid. According to researchers at the University of Surrey, as reported in the *Journal of Environmental Psychology*, resistance to change remains a continuing challenge: "Past behaviour or habit, and psychological reactance, have been explored as components of resistance. Growing evidence for the influence of self-identity on behaviour suggests self-identity as a further factor." How we see ourselves is the largest contributing factor to how greatly we resist change; it's even more significant than our past behavior. We are scared to make change because our identity will also change and we have fear around loss.

We usually see our identity as being fixed. For many women, it's defined by our roles and responsibilities, especially in relation to others. Our essence is always unfolding, and we need to remember we are meant to evolve. We will experience many new versions of ourselves in our lifetimes, each one serving a profound purpose until we outgrow it over time. We are always in the process of becoming, and there is no final destination.

When we have outgrown our past yet still define ourselves with those labels, we often wait way too long for change as we live incongruently without even realizing it. The reason we don't feel like ourselves is because we have outgrown our past labels. Our needs, desires, and preferences have changed. A new mold is waiting, one that fits us better.

How we define ourselves can be limiting and feed into limiting beliefs. What are the qualities or labels that you can shed to help you step into your new identity? When we are around different people and in different environments, our identities change. We adapt who we are to fit the mold required. Motivational speaker Jim Rohn suggests that we are the average of the five people we spend the most time with. It's important that we can strive to be ourselves and have internal alignment, regardless of who those five people may be.

Acting boldly is doing things differently and learning to trust yourself in the process as you honor your needs, values, and vision.

Swiss psychiatrist Carl Jung theorized that there are archetypes that come from the collective unconscious; these models are innate, universal, unlearned, and hereditary. Archetypes organize how we experience certain things. In *Verywell Mind*, the four main archetypes he identified are:

1. **The Persona:** How we present ourselves to the outside world—our mask.

2. **The Shadow:** Sexual and survival instincts that exist in the unconscious mind—what we repress.

3. **The Anima/Animus:** The masculine and feminine parts of the psyche in the collective unconscious.

4. **The Self:** The unified unconscious and conscious self.

Genevieve's persona was a "good" wife and mother. Her shadow comprised the fears and disappointments she repressed. Her animus was urging her to break free from fear and survival mode. The woman she was stepping into was the self—herself.

We know ourselves one way and yet we are moving away from that into the unknown. That's why we are fearful as we approach change. Our identity is shifting, which can feel scary and exciting at the same time. The same physiological experience is happening in your body when you experience fear and excitement, and it's up to you to label it. So, will you give yourself some grace? Will you choose to be excited for your new identity to be revealed?

How we view ourselves is a self-constructed reality. In *The Self Illusion*, Bruce Hood argues that the "notion of the independent, coherent self is an illusion—it is not what it seems. Reality as we perceive it is not something that objectively exists, but something that our brains construct from moment to moment, interpreting, summarizing, and substituting information along the way." Our past experiences form our reality and give us the illusion of a stable self. How we perceive our identity is shaped by our brains making up stories and labels about who we are, without our conscious awareness.

Hood explains how the idea of self begins in childhood as the architecture of the developing brain enables us to connect with others. He explains that our idea of ourselves is the product of our relationships and interactions with others, and yet it *only* exists in our brains. Our identity is a construct, a mere illusion; it is not permanent. It's meant to evolve. This is good news: it means you get to intentionally define the next version of yourself.

No one likes uncertainty, and change always involves uncertainty, which is why we stay stuck. Dr. Maya Shankar is a cognitive scientist who studies human behavior and unexpected change. Her studies suggest that we avoid the unexpected because of how we are wired: "Research shows that we're more stressed when we're told we have a 50 percent chance of getting an electric shock than when we're told we have a 100 percent chance." As humans, we like to know outcomes so strongly that we would prefer to be certain a bad thing will happen than accept it's only a possibility. No wonder we avoid making changes.

But, my friend, there is always a cost to waiting. Living out of alignment, out of integrity, and out of balance with our mind, body, and soul for a long time has a significant cost to our well-being. The cost of waiting is always at the expense of living. We sacrifice internal peace by waiting for change; instead, you can make the decision to change and regain your peace in the process.

When you wait for things to get better, you are not attending to your own needs, desires, and dreams. Constantly neglecting yourself is not called living; it's called existing. If you are only going through the motions of life but want more, this is your invitation to wake up and stop waiting.

High-stakes change that alters our identity moves us from an old way of being into a new way. Shankar states that we become different people on the other side of change, by learning what we are capable of, what we value, and how we define ourselves. So often we only see the setbacks, limitations, and fears, rather than the gifts that change can bring. Shankar encourages us to focus on the expansiveness of change and provides three questions to ask ourselves:

1. What do you think you are capable of?
2. What do you value right now in your life?
3. How do you define yourself right now?

Reflecting on these questions will lead you to a new way of thinking about change.

I invite you to reflect on what stuck-on labels you need to peel off yourself. Labels like good Christian, faithful wife, or dutiful daughter-in-law may be standing in your way and may no longer serve you. Ask yourself what qualities, like being loyal or hardworking, can continue to be congruent and intact even as your identity, roles, or relationships change.

Our perception of our identity and how we define ourselves impact our actions. Ask yourself who you want to become and give yourself permission to change. Go through the Get Unstuck, Cycle of Change Model knowing that it's healthy to change, that fear is part of the process, and that when you act boldly, you will meet the next version of you. Life is not meant to be static. It's okay to remove old labels and acquire new roles, relationships, and beliefs. Hanging on to past labels prevents you from experiencing your greatest future.

Eckhart Tolle, spiritual teacher and self-help author, states, "Any action is often better than no action, especially if you have been stuck in an unhappy situation for a long time. If it is a mistake, at least you learn something, in which case it's no longer a mistake. If you remain stuck, you learn nothing."

Give yourself permission to make the change you desire; even if you make a mistake, as Tolle says, you move forward and you learn. It's in the boldness of stepping outside your comfort zone that you will learn about yourself, step into your next version, and create an identity that serves you. Learning more about yourself always gives you power.

The Power of Choice

In 1946, Viktor Frankl, Austrian psychiatrist and Holocaust survivor, wrote *Man's Search for Meaning,* inspiring this quotation: "Between stimulus and response lies a space. In that space lie our freedom and power to choose our response. In our response lies our growth and our happiness."

We always have the power of choice. We get to decide how we respond; what our attitude toward any circumstance, situation, or change is; and who to become. Once we understand how fear is holding us back, we get the opportunity to respond. Frankl wrote, "When we are no longer able to change a situation... we are challenged to change ourselves." So instead of continuing to wait for a situation to change, it's up to us to change within ourselves.

Change may not always seem fair, but there is a silver lining: we get to become more of the person we were meant to be. Change allows us to be molded, as heat does to iron. Iron needs to get hot before it can be molded into the masterpiece it is destined to be. Fear is the heat required for transformation, to allow for the next version of ourselves to take shape.

Genevieve had the power of choice for many years, though she was oblivious to it because she was living in fear. All she could see were the obstacles, which kept her feeling stuck. However, even in the hardest situations, we get to decide what will happen for the rest of our life.

When we decide to lean into fear, rather than avoid it, we learn to trust ourselves. When a relationship ends because we finally choose to take care of our own needs and put boundaries in place, we honor our feelings, hopes, and desires. We can recognize it was a relationship built on self-abandonment. When you dishonor yourself and stay silent so as not to rock the boat in a relationship, you are subconsciously telling yourself you are not worthy and your needs don't matter.

This is your invitation to take bold action and step outside your comfort zone, to move beyond what you thought was possible. This is your opportunity to do what you have been avoiding or what you have been waiting to feel ready for.

The Ability to Surrender

When the pain of the present exceeds the pain of making a change for the future, most people are forced into action. When you stop resisting and start accepting your reality, you learn the art of surrender. Can you surrender to yourself as you are now?

I like to think of surrender as the deliberate intention to make change, trusting yourself in the process. Surrender is not complacency. Surrender is accepting what is happening in your life as it is in order to release the aspects that you want to leave in the past.

Let's take a moment to imagine what your life could look like if you took the necessary steps forward into your new identity with more ease and less fear. Visualize surrendering what you had planned for your life and accepting what is happening in your life. Surrendering can bring you to a place of internal alignment and peace. Yes, it's hard, and it's a practice.

Sometimes we won't understand the reason for change in our life until after the fact. As my beloved grandma Poochie used to say, "It's always in the hindsight that we can make sense of our lives and connect the dots and the reason behind the changes in our lives." Choosing flow over force and expansion over contraction always serves our mind, body, and soul.

Mind, Body, and Soul Action Steps

Most people focus solely on the things they *must* do and the behaviors and action steps required to make change. Very few consider how change impacts their entire being. Like Genevieve, who was so focused on the question of leaving her marriage, she forgot to give attention to the changes that would occur in her mind, body, and soul. To ensure that our action steps support our vision for life, we need to get specific on how they impact us mentally, physically, and emotionally.

Perhaps you don't think you have time to process your feelings and want to focus on the concrete act of making change. According to Harvard-trained neuroanatomist Dr. Jill Bolte Taylor, it takes us ninety seconds to identify an emotion and allow it to dissipate through our body as we simply notice it. It only takes ninety seconds to complete your body's physiological response process; it's such a short amount of time to sit in discomfort, but we often resist and block emotions, unwilling to endure it. When our body experiences change and stress, it's important to honor each emotion so we can move through to the other side of change.

Give yourself permission to feel fear, and also give yourself permission to feel proud, brave, positive, and powerful on the other side of making change. Properly preparing yourself for what will unfold in your mind, body, and soul helps you feel empowered.

Our soul is where we receive confirmation that we are on the right path, with a lightness and peace surrounding us. Our soul is what comes to life when we take aligned action. We get confirmation as we tap into our wisdom and listen to our intuition, learning to trust ourselves with each step we take. We move from a place of fear to a place of faith. You can't live in both places at once.

Embrace Your Fear and Know It's Part of the Process

Fear is real for all of us, and it can get in the way of making significant change. This is normal, and you are normal. Choose to embrace fear and hold space for it. Don't avoid it; lean into fear and hold it close like a newborn baby, in awe of what it will become. When you experience fear, it's a cue to move forward, not a sign to back down.

Getting your mind, body, and soul into unison gives you momentum like you have never experienced before, and you will need courage to access connection and alignment with yourself. It's important to distinguish between what it means to "take action" and to "take aligned action." Usually we can all take some sort of action and do things to make our life better. Aligned action means serving your highest self and your highest potential, with steps that are in tune with your core values, vision, and needs to support you over the long term. Aligned action serves you and supports who you are and what you stand for. Imagine your ninety-year-old self speaking with you today. What would she say to you to help you take your next step? Focus on that.

Aligned action is about intentionally saying yes to the right things. When you say yes to things that are out of alignment with your vision and values, you are saying no to yourself. Over time, you program yourself to believe you are unworthy because you have not honored the essence of who you are. Aligned action whispers to you, encourages you, and reaffirms that you are on the right path, even though you don't know the entire path. Your intuition speaks up and directs you as you take aligned action. Aligned action opens up opportunities beyond what you can imagine. It's not possible to experience aligned action without truly knowing yourself and considering the mind, body, and soul action steps. When you have this kind of clarity, you learn to trust yourself and act boldly.

Stay Accountable to Yourself in the Process

Genevieve made a promise to herself that she would do everything she possibly could to make her marriage work. When she was out of resources and exhausted from the hurt and disappointment of trying, she knew it was time to surrender and let go. She had given her marriage her best shot, so she would have no regrets.

When Genevieve acknowledged that it was not only on her to make her marriage work, since it was a partnership that both people needed to make effort in, she gave herself permission to adopt a new perspective. In the process, her mind strengthened, her body regained energy, and her soul felt free; she returned back to herself. Giving yourself permission to adjust your plans in order to stay true to yourself is key to the journey of change and to experiencing the full beauty of life.

In time, Genevieve met a better version of herself and liked her more. She took three months away to travel all around Europe, enjoying fine wines and culture, and she completed some items that brought her joy on her newly made bucket list. She learned how to be alone but not feel lonely. All the pieces of her were put back together in a more magnificent way to fit who she was now.

A year after her divorce, we met up for coffee. After catching up, she told me something massive.

"I'm taking burlesque dancing."

My jaw dropped. "Wow, Genevieve, you really are next level." I cheered for her.

"I have never felt so scared and alive at the same time. I felt liberated. I had no idea I could be this brave and bold."

"That is bold," I said. "You are brave." I couldn't believe what she'd just shared.

She gave me the biggest smile I've ever seen from her. "I found myself again, and I love this version better. I know it's okay for me to see myself again and not hide behind fear anymore."

She had wanted to break free from her body insecurities once and for all. She wanted to enjoy herself, including what she looked like physically, so she deliberately did something that scared her in a big way. By embracing fear, she would set herself free. It turned out that by hitting a pose onstage in skin-tight black leather leggings and a form-fitting black top, she found her light again, which no one could take from her again. She was no longer in the wings in her own life, peeking out and waiting for change. She had found her courage and stepped out of her comfort zone into her next version of herself. She let go, and she let herself live more fully.

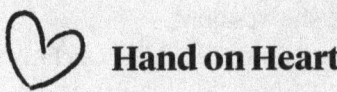 **Hand on Heart**

Say this out loud to affirm yourself:

It's safe to act boldly and step outside my comfort zone even when I don't feel ready. I can trust myself, and I can figure things out as I go along. I am ready to embrace the next version of myself, and I understand that not everything and everyone will fit with the new person I am becoming.

Place your hand on your heart, take deep breaths, and ask yourself these questions:

Where am I out of alignment with myself right now?

What am I avoiding out of fear?

Will this change bring alignment into my life?

How can I prepare my mind, body, and soul for the change I am making?

P.S. You can learn to make fear your dance partner. Taking a bold step may not feel the way you anticipate it will, but that's a good thing...

8
JOY IN THE JOURNEY

"The secret of change is to focus all your energy not on fighting the old, but on building the new."

DAN MILLMAN

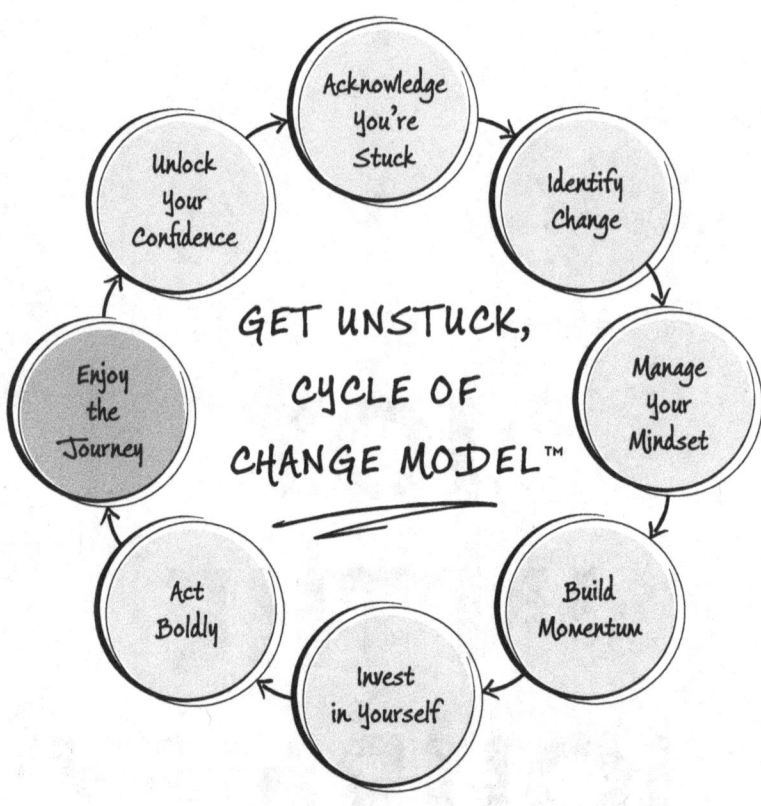

Now that you have acted boldly and stepped outside your comfort zone, it's time to give yourself permission to enjoy the journey. You have done the work, and now you'll make space to be intentional about enjoyment. Take some time to feel the pleasure of making change!

ANIKA REALLY NEEDED permission to experience joy in the midst of making change. She is a woman who gets shit done. She gets more done in a day than most people do in a week. If she was on your team, you would want her to take on all the most important projects.

But you could never get her on your team because she's quite content to pour her effort into building her empire of not one, not two, but *three* highly successful and profitable businesses, each in a different industry.

In my experience, when faced with a BFC in life, roughly 95 percent of people get stuck in overthinking, cling to the edges of their comfort zones, and fail to take the necessary action to make change. They fail to embrace the next version of themselves and live with dissatisfaction and regret. That's why I wrote this book.

Anika is part of the other 5 percent. She loves taking action and being in perpetual motion. I'm not even sure she knows what a comfort zone is. She enjoys stretching herself beyond her limits and trying new things, even when something scares the crap out of her. *Especially* when something scares the crap out of her. She rarely overthinks and is constantly switching things up in her life and in her businesses. Change is part of her identity.

Unlike most of us, change motivates her; it makes her feel alive and excited about the future. The thought of staying stagnant, static, or the same makes her deeply unhappy and uncomfortable.

In her personal life, this shows up as traveling all over the world, moving to different countries, changing gyms just to "switch it up," and learning new skills "just because." In her businesses, she is always trying new models, processes, and systems, and she takes big risks.

As a result, Anika has enjoyed a success that most other entrepreneurs, especially women, only dream of.

On the surface, it looks like Anika is an action-taker in every area of her life. But, like many people in the 5 percent, she is driven by a story buried deep inside. External success has proven to be an antidote to a problem that plagued her as a child and teenager, one that is deeply ingrained in the hearts of many girls and women: she feels like she is not enough. She feels remarkably unremarkable. She spent much of her childhood feeling unseen and unnoticed by her teachers and peers, never quite fitting in. Never feeling that she belonged, and only feeling like an outsider looking in.

"Is it because I'm not pretty enough?" she would wonder. "Or because I'm not smart enough? Nor funny or cool enough?"

Over time, her sense of being not enough became a subtle but constant presence in her life. She found a way to silence that voice by proving it wrong with every new success she achieved. She learned that she could *earn* her way to being enough, success by success, dollar by dollar, and accolade by accolade.

It worked as long as her projects were succeeding, her businesses growing, her net worth increasing. But the moment she experienced anything she would consider a failure, including relatively minor setbacks, she was filled with the sense—the *knowing*—that she was not enough, not worthy of being valued. So, she made a business out of busyness. She was addicted to making changes and made more BFCs than anyone I've ever met. In my experience, most people have a maximum of ten BFCs in a lifetime; she's already had at least twenty and is only in her late forties. This woman is unstoppable.

After Anika learned she had an aptitude for business, she had subconsciously tied her sense of worth, and in some way her identity, to her career outcomes. It was her way to process her pain, a coping mechanism she had learned over the years in her effort to feel she was enough. That connection was reinforced by the admiration and respect that others gave her in response to her success. She was proud of herself and what she had achieved on her own. She put blood, sweat, and tears into building her empire. She often wondered why other people didn't do more in life and couldn't understand why change was hard for them. She was stuck in *doing* mode all the time with no off button to be found.

To the outside world, she shines like a diamond, but on the inside, she is perpetually running away from the fear that she is unpolished and unfinished. She is well connected but doesn't feel as if she is. She seems confident and self-assured in the eyes of others, but she's deeply uncomfortable in silence. She seems to have an endless supply of energy, but she's internally exhausted by the hamster wheel of validation by way of success. There is no exit door: once she stops moving, once she stops achieving, her positive feelings quickly evaporate, along with the identity she worked hard to build. She is tied to what she does, not who she is.

This happens to many of us. I could relate to Anika: I would feel amazing when I landed the lead dance roles and would feel less than when I did not. What I accomplished and the accolades I received molded my identity as a dancer. I experienced more or less joy based on the role I was cast in and where I was positioned onstage. I felt good when my businesses were thriving, my dancers winning, and my clients succeeding. The contrary was true as well. I have learned the importance of separating my work and my roles from who I am as a person.

Many high achievers attach their identities to what they *accomplish* rather than *who* they are. Don't get me wrong: it's amazing to achieve and be ambitious as long as we stay grounded in who we are regardless of external circumstances and validation. When we no longer need to share the highs and lows with others and can process the wins and losses on our own, we don't define ourselves by what we do but rather who we are. This is a sweet spot to be in, because you can achieve and succeed or fail and reflect without it defining who you are. Ambition and achievements are amazing as long as you still have a sense of self with or without them.

Tying your sense of identity to your outcomes is a dangerous game, one that works really well until it doesn't. This is especially true when you are as competent and determined as Anika. She doesn't focus on feelings; she focuses on action.

Here's the thing. In this book, I have been encouraging you to take action toward a big change that is meaningful and pivotal, that shifts your identity in positive ways. But sometimes we can make really big changes and still identify with old stories at our core. Even when we've achieved the *external* changes successfully, we don't *feel* the way we hoped to when we set out to make the BFC in the first place. Or if we do feel it, it's only temporary, and we soon find ourselves back in old ways of feeling, confused about why we aren't happier, more satisfied, and more positive. That's what was happening for Anika. She could achieve anything, but she stopped feeling joy, she forgot to celebrate, and she was in a constant search for the next dopamine hit.

When we are making a BFC in our lives, we are very often trying to change our own sense of self in the process. Some of us are aware of this, but for most of us, it is unknown. For change to be successful, our sense of self has to be flexible enough to make the shift, and the new identity needs to be more attractive than the old one to motivate the change. Otherwise, we stay stuck. Stuck with our old identity and stuck wanting a new one. We miss our lives and our moments, because nothing feels quite right. We only go through the motions. We stop feeling alive and we fail to have joy in the journey. When making a BFC, we need to understand *why* we want to make the change. Getting attached to the feeling, and not the outcome, is key.

In many cases, our old sense of identity has been very effective at providing us with a feeling of belonging and connection with those around us, and it can be hard to let go of that, even when it's the right thing to do. It makes us feel uncomfortable because it is outside our comfort zone. When we truly believe in the core of our being that our new identity is a better path to that belonging and connection, we will allow those internal changes to happen. We all want to feel seen, heard, loved, valued, and accepted. We are all wired for connection, and the most valuable connection is the one within ourselves. But most of us forget about the connection to self as we wear so many different hats in our lives.

If our being and our doing are not aligned, we will either end up not making the change, or making it but feeling dissatisfied. If you've ever said some version of "I thought I would feel happier if I changed jobs, but I still feel unfulfilled" or "I thought I would feel different, but I feel the same," you have experienced this.

As Reverend Rick Warren shared in *The Purpose Driven Life*, "We are human *beings*, not human *doings*." Our being is where our identity truly resides, and the doing is just an expression of that. What you do matters, but how you do it matters more. If you understand the reason for making the change, you are most likely to experience alignment within yourself.

If we ignore our being on our way to doing, we may still achieve external success, make external changes and lots of BFCs, but it will never feel quite right. We will stay unfulfilled, disconnected, and lost. Something will feel off. The dopamine hit will wear off and we'll wonder why we are not happy. We won't experience the joy of success, and we certainly won't enjoy the process.

To find joy in the journey, we have to create alignment between our doing and being—what we do and who we are need to complement each other. This is where everything comes together: we feel connected in our mind, body, and soul. It's important to enjoy your life and take time to enjoy the journey. Find some joy in the journey of your life.

Flipping the Script

The key to creating that alignment, and to enjoying both the journey and the benefits of our BFCs, is to understand that we are all operating from scripts (or old stories) that tell us how to think about ourselves and how to act in different situations. We touched on this earlier with limiting beliefs, archetypes, and labels, but now you're ready to go deeper and think about the stories that run automatically in your mind.

Here's the deal: sometimes those scripts are really helpful, and sometimes they aren't. In the latter case, to move forward, we need to flip the script. Start by paying attention to the voices in your head and then choose to replace them. Flipping the script starts with internal awareness. Pay attention to what you repeatedly say to yourself, and take a moment to realize whose voice each story is echoing. I hear "Money does not grow on trees" thanks to my dad and "Always be kind" thanks to my mom. The voices that are programmed into our minds make an impact on how we show up in the world. I definitely have both of those voices in my mind, which are helpful, but there are also ones that are not serving me.

Here are the three steps to flipping a script:

1 **Identify Your Core Script:** What story plays on repeat in your mind? For example, "I will never be good enough," "I will always be overweight," or "nothing good ever happens to me."

2 **Determine How That Script Serves You:** How is the script keeping you safe and keeping you playing small? Is it holding you back from stepping outside your comfort zone?

3 **Rewrite the Script:** Replace the old script with a story that supports the woman you are becoming and the new version of yourself. Focus on the who, what, where, when, and why in your description. Give yourself time to reflect on these questions to gain clarity. For example, "I have always been good enough, though I sometimes didn't see it."

Identifying Your Core Script

Most of our scripts were written long ago when we were children, and we've been playing them out ever since. In healthy environments, those scripts are extremely helpful as we learn how to act, especially in relation to others, and adapt to new situations. These scripts can help us make the BFCs we want in our lives. We know what to do and how to act. But in unhealthy environments, those scripts aren't very adaptive to change. Unfortunately, some of us are unaware that we were in unhealthy environments and are still unaware of the negative scripts playing on repeat. They often will show up in relationships with others and be brought to the surface in times of conflict.

The best way to determine which scripts serve us and which ones limit us is to listen for negative or critical voices in our heads, especially when we try to step out of our comfort zones. Pay attention to the voice that comes up when you are taking on risk, when you are doing something out of the ordinary, and when you are being brave, positive, powerful, and bold. Become curious about that story's origin and whose voice you hear inside your head. You may hear a parent's, friend's, or teacher's voice in your head. You may be surprised by whose voice it is. Most people have not reflected on this before, so this awareness can give you profound clarity. The unkind voices in our heads are always scripts worth flipping. *Always.*

Write down the criticism that feels the most painful and that you hear most frequently. *That is likely your core script.* It needs an update and some love. Ask yourself, "What else is possible?" and repeat a new script at least a few times each day to start training your brain to think in a different way. Reframing, repeating, and reprogramming can shift your internal world in a big way, so that the next version of yourself is more expansive. As you grow, your scripts also need to evolve.

Your connection to yourself is the most important, and it is mirrored in your relationships with others. Pay attention to your judging mind. When you judge others negatively, you are often noticing insecurities within yourself. When you admire others, they often display a trait you wish to develop. When we are judgmental or admiring of others, we often have the same trait within us. For example, if we say a person is lazy, we could have an insecurity about not being productive or pride ourselves on how much we can accomplish in a day. Our vantage point is always based on our strengths and weaknesses. See what comes up for you; this is an opportunity to grow.

Determine How That Script Serves You

Once you've identified your core script and noticed the effect it's having in your life, it can be tempting to view it as something bad that needs to be discarded. Try to avoid all-or-nothing thinking. Not everything is black and white; gray exists everywhere. While this script may now be negatively impacting in your life, you adopted this script as a method to cope with past challenges. It is how you made sense of your world and it served an important role for a period of time. It may still be serving you in some important ways, even if its overall effect on your life is negative. If you try to remove your core script without *understanding its purpose,* and how it may still be serving you, you will be unsuccessful. It will continue to play on repeat in your mind. Understanding how it helped you will help you heal, let go, and "release it with love," as I like to say. Then you can find a healthier, more mature, and more adaptive replacement for it. It can be as simple as replacing "I suck at this" with "I am becoming better at this."

The key is to approach the internal conversation with compassion, love, and gratitude and without judgment or resistance. Let it come up so you can let it go out. You need to go through hard emotions to create new long-lasting positive scripts. Only under those conditions can you move forward to the next step, which is to love ourselves more, let go of the people we were, and step into the people we are becoming.

Update the Script with a New Version

Updating your scripts helps unlock your confidence. Take a few minutes to think about potential ways to address the concerns that came up for you. If you get it wrong, that's okay. You can try again. You can always update this script again. It is a journey. Strive for progress, not perfection, one step at a time.

With an understanding of the role your core script is playing in your life, let's look at some potential replacements that are more suited to who you are now and who you want to become.

It's said that a habit is a hard thing to break, and a thought habit is even harder as it's been programmed into us without our awareness. With my limiting belief that I was not brilliant, I had to work hard to replace it with new thoughts and new scripts. Thought habits take time, intention, and awareness to change. Intentionally working to flip the script is a really good start, and it's sometimes enough to adopt a new script permanently. But it's often necessary to remind ourselves over a period of time of our updated script.

Repetition is our friend, so let's use it to our advantage. As a dancer and teacher, my go-to phrase is "Let's do it one more time." We are always on repeat until we lock it in. A great way to lock in with repetition is to tape your script of how you want to feel about yourself to your bathroom mirror. Every morning when you get up, and every night when you go to sleep, put your hand on your heart and read the script out loud to yourself for yourself. You will notice shifts in your energy and your confidence. This simple exercise reprograms your mind, body, and soul. You will feel more comfortable letting go to let in.

If this is hard for you, it's okay! That just means you're normal. We all experience resistance in different areas of our lives. Ultimately, it's a sign that our being and our doing are not yet aligned. You know you can *do* anything, but you may be lacking in the *being* part of life. If you have thought, "Why is this so hard?" or "Why am I not happy?" or "What's wrong with me?" you definitely have some scripts that need to be flipped by focusing on your feelings and the being part of you.

It's always easier to identify external changes than to realize the internal changes that are deeply ingrained and need to be replaced. Yes, it's easier to blame others and look outside ourselves. Brené Brown, researcher, professor, and speaker, says, "Authenticity is the daily practice of letting go of who we think we're supposed to be and embracing who we are."

We want more out of life. And we can have it. And you now have a pathway to experience alignment and reveal your authentic self.

Once you make the changes you want, you may feel different than you expected, which is a sign that you have grown through the process of change. Change changes you. As a result of your growth, your needs, desires, and preferences have evolved. What used to meet your needs or make you feel good might no longer, and that's okay. Just be mindful of how you feel, so you don't get discouraged or move backward by relying on outdated scripts as the new version of yourself is trying to emerge.

When you achieve your goal, it may not be exactly what you hoped or imagined. It may be more than you could have anticipated, different, or disappointing. Remember that you made the change and achieved your result, which is a win. Celebrate it and celebrate yourself and keep moving forward.

You stepped out and tapped into courage to make your BFC, and it can feel discouraging to know that feeling discouraged can be *part*

It's okay to start over or change directions at any age, at any time, for any reason.

of the process. You see, as you uplevel your life, your goals, vision, and values reset; you get used to the changes, and that becomes your new baseline. And with this new baseline, we can experience discontentment again. This is part of the human experience, and it happens to all of us. Dissatisfaction is a motivator for growth. Don't be discouraged by it; get determined and keep moving forward one step at a time.

Permission Granted

If you are still standing on the edge but need a little more of a push before taking the leap, you may be waiting to give yourself permission. Yup, we all seek permission and often look externally for it. But all along you've held the key. Here is your gentle nudge, the cue you have been waiting for, your tap on the shoulder. Give yourself permission and go and step out of the wings. I like to say "permission granted" before I make a significant change. Say it out loud and give yourself permission. Permission is granted for you to make your BFC and to enjoy the journey as well. It's okay if you don't do it perfectly, or if you change directions a few times before you find your pathway. It's about stepping out to step up.

If you are still feeling stuck, even with your new skills, tools, resources, and understanding of the Get Unstuck, Cycle of Change Model, don't despair. This usually means you really need to give yourself permission to change. I am not talking about permission from others, but permission from *yourself*. You may be standing in your own way unable to move forward.

As children, we were conditioned to seek permission or advice about what to do or how to behave, especially in uncertain times, so it's natural that we look outside ourselves for approval and permission. We need to become the seekers of our lives and discover our own truths. No one lives your life except you. No one knows you better than you. And no one knows your potential, desires, and dreams better than you. Sometimes, you just need to let go of what you thought your life would look like and open up to what your life is becoming. Give yourself permission to change directions, make a new decision, live a different life, break societal norms, and choose a path to self-discovery and alignment.

The beautifully unfinished messy middle is where we feel lost, stuck, disconnected, and unfulfilled. It's also what you experience before you find yourself again and meet the next version of yourself. If you can accept what is, you can give yourself permission to make change. Sometimes taking a hard, loving look at reality helps you grant yourself permission. Letting go of what was and your hopes and dreams is hard. It's devastating, and it's necessary for you to step into who you are meant to be.

It's okay to start over or change directions at any age, at any time, for any reason. It's okay to try again, and it's okay to give yourself permission to change as many times as needed, whenever you need. You didn't fail. You course corrected. You made a necessary pivot, and you still have lots of life ahead of you. Focus on what's ahead and who you are becoming. Sometimes you need to cut your losses and go, before you get stuck in the comfort and company of misery.

If you are like me, you may be looking for the perfect decision and the ideal time to get the best result, which sadly don't exist. Sometimes you just need to make a move and give yourself permission to adjust as many times as needed without getting things perfectly. Trust your intuition and adjust your path accordingly. Remember there is joy in the journey. Even the bumps and detours can be gifts when you are open to receive them.

Your Next Version Is Waiting for You

Congratulations, you are stepping into the next version of yourself. You have done all the waiting. The next version of you is here waiting for you. Your life is waiting for you, your potential is waiting for you, and the world is waiting for you to share your gifts. Choose you and choose to believe in your highest potential. Be dedicated to doing the work to find all of yourself again—even the new parts you haven't met. You are never done growing, and you'll always be in the stage of becoming. Take it all in. Breathe it in. Surrender to what is, as that is the only place where *being* truly exists. Accept, embrace, and love yourself and your life.

Something is calling you to become a new version of yourself. You know what you want, and it's here for you—take it. Grab it with both hands, and know that you are worthy of it. Whatever your *it* may be. You deserve it. You are not too much, and you are more than enough. Enjoy changing, and go through the change. You don't need to feel ready; your confidence will come after you make the change.

 Hand on Heart

Say this out loud to affirm yourself:

I am loved. I love myself. I am love. I choose to lean into the vibrational state of love. I am worthy of love and deserving of love. I am enough today, tomorrow, and always.

Close your eyes, place your hand on your heart, take deep breaths, and ask yourself these questions:

How can I love myself more?

I am capable. What quality do I want to strengthen?

I have unlocked my confidence. How do I protect my confidence more?

I will find joy in the journey. How can I celebrate more?

P.S. You may not feel as you expected, because you've outgrown the old version of yourself, which is a positive thing. It's okay if you are still not feeling confident. You will unlock this next.

9
UNLOCK YOUR CONFIDENCE

*"Your success will be determined
by your own confidence and fortitude."*

MICHELLE OBAMA

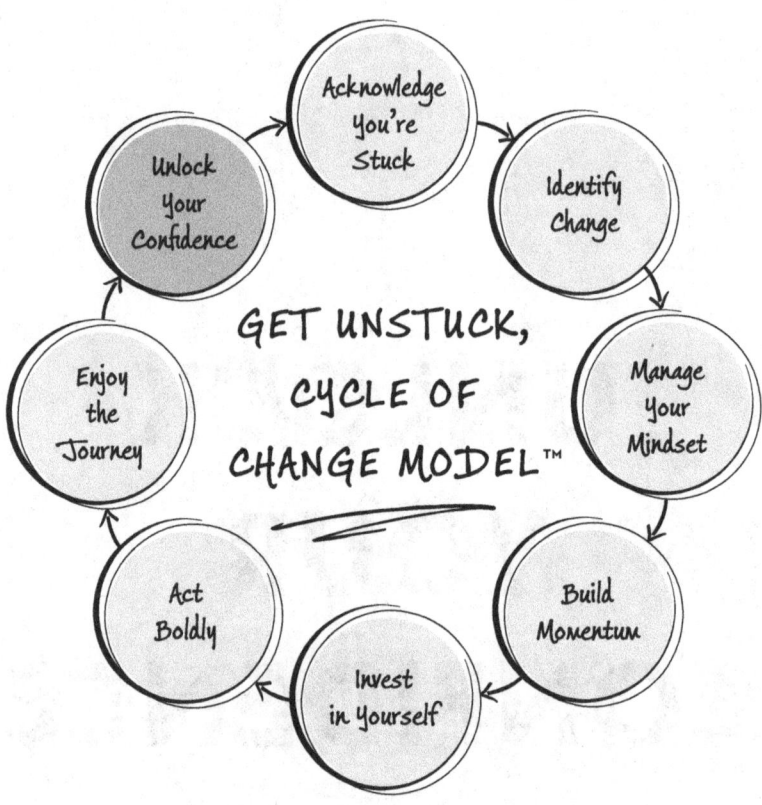

Congratulations! You're here! You've made it to the final step in the Get Unstuck, Cycle of Change Model. You are now unlocking your confidence—your reward for doing the hard work. You have changed, and you're stepping into the next version of yourself. High five and fist pump to you!

WILMA WAS A bright and hardworking administrative assistant in her mid-thirties, working for a small party-planning company. She hired me as a coach to help her improve her communication skills. She felt unable to articulate her perspectives to her boss, Gerry, in a way that would be received, even when it was clear to her that the company would benefit from her suggestions. She had a lot of experience in the event industry and was extremely organized with a keen eye for detail, but she didn't feel valued by the people she worked for. She was treated more like a part of a machine than the asset she was.

Every time Wilma tried to speak up, she was ignored or dismissed, and it was starting to affect her confidence. Over time, her internal conflict grew and was eating her up. As a child, her core script was that she was to be seen, not heard, and that her opinion really didn't matter. Gerry didn't appreciate her input, and his expectations of her were often unrealistic, which led to frustration on both sides. To compensate, Wilma worked longer hours under a lot of pressure; she was getting dangerously close to a breaking point and was suffering from anxiety attacks.

Watching the frustration overwhelm her, I asked, "How do you think you can address this problem?"

"Well, I need to tell Gerry that his timelines are *completely* unreasonable."

"That sounds easy enough," I said. "So, what's stopping you from doing that?"

"He'll just tell me that it's urgent, and that it has to be done *yesterday*, and then get mad at me for not being a team player."

I dug a little deeper. "Okay, so if he gets mad, what will happen?"

Her shoulders tensed, and her breathing became shallow. "For starters, I'll probably lose my job. And then I won't be able to pay my rent, so I'll lose my apartment."

"No wonder you're afraid to speak up," I said. "What would happen if you didn't say anything?"

"Everything will stay the same. I'll feel stuck and stressed out. And he'll probably keep thinking that I'm the problem. And I'm not the problem. He'd be *screwed* without me. I keep everything running smoothly. If I try defending myself at all, he'll get angry, and I'll probably lose my job. I just can't win here!"

"Let me make sure that I'm understanding the situation, okay?"

She nodded.

"Either you *don't* speak up, Gerry moves forward with unrealistic expectations, and then fires you for not meeting them, or... you *do* speak up, he gets mad at you for not being a team player, and then he fires you. You'll lose your job and then you'll lose your apartment. Am I missing anything?"

"Nope. That's exactly the problem."

I smiled and said, "Well, that's awesome, Wilma! You are in such an incredible position right now!"

"Wait, what? I don't think you understand, Cara. I'm in a *horrible* position! No matter what, I lose!"

"Exactly!" I said. "I wonder if we could look at this a *little bit differently*, from the opposite end. Can we try?"

She nodded.

"You *feel* like no matter what you do in this situation, you lose, but from my perspective you are in the perfect situation to gain. Based on what you're telling me, you actually have nothing to lose. This is the perfect time to make a Big Freakin' Change.

"So far, you have tried saying nothing, pushing down your feelings, staying small, and working harder to try to achieve the impossible, all the while sacrificing your own peace and happiness."

"Yes, that's exactly right."

"Okay. You have also tried your best to manage his expectations around your workload. You've worked ridiculously long hours. You've skipped your lunches, been overcaffeinated, and dug in your heels to try to meet his deadlines. None of that is working. And since that's *not* working, it's a sign that the only possible solution left is to do the opposite. What is the opposite of what you've been doing?"

"Well," she pondered, "I guess the opposite would be to have an honest conversation with him, but I really don't know how to do that."

"You have acknowledged that you're stuck, identified you need to make a career change, managed your mindset, built some momentum, invested in yourself—and now it's time to act boldly. This will help you enjoy your life and your work more, savoring the journey and truly unlocking your confidence," I said, reminding Wilma of all of the work she had already completed.

Wilma hired me to help her with her communication because she believed that she had simply not been communicating effectively with her boss and that she was the problem. But in reality, she had stopped communicating altogether out of fear of losing her job. She stopped trusting herself to use her voice, and as a result, she was unwittingly *perpetuating* the cycle instead of solving it. Wilma was actually an excellent communicator, but she had slowly allowed a lack of confidence to creep in, and that kept her stuck in an unsustainable situation. She lost her voice in the process of trying harder.

"Let's talk about the possible results of having the hard conversation. The worst-case scenario is that you'll get fired for speaking up. What do you think the *best*-case scenario could be?"

"Well, I guess the best-case scenario is that that he would listen to my input and give me a little more breathing room."

"Great. What would be even better than that?" I asked.

She paused. "Gerry would *actually* respect me enough to let me decide on how my work should be done."

We were starting to bump into the limits of her confidence. I said, "You'd like to be listened to, have realistic expectations for your work, and be respected. What would make this situation even better?"

"Um," she said meekly, "well, to be honest, I'd like to earn a bit more money." This is how BFC's work, they set other changes and possibilities into motion too, in this case financial.

"Awesome, so the best-case scenario is that you are listened to, respected, have reasonable expectations set, and get paid more money. What else?"

"I don't think anything else would be realistic, Cara. I get what you're trying to do, but I also have to be *re-a-lis-tic*!" Wilma drew out the last word as if it carried more weight than all the others combined.

"Realism is just a container for what we imagine is possible, Wilma. Trust me on this. If we expand the container of our imagination to include the things that we don't *yet* believe are possible, our lives will also expand to make room for more. It's okay to think beyond what you believe to be possible. So... what *else*?"

There was long silence as she mentally pushed up against the edges of her comfort zone.

A tear formed in the corner of her right eye. "I'm just so tired of working for someone else, Cara. All I *really* want is to be my own boss. I want to work for myself. I want to work for *myself*!" Wilma covered her hands over her mouth in shock as her eyes widened. "Oh my gosh, I've never said that before. I don't even know where that *came* from."

I smiled. "Okay, now we are talking. What does it *feel* like to be your own boss?" She was now talking about an intellectual change as well.

"It feels like I have a voice," Wilma said. "Like I can create my own life, one that feels powerful." She sat up taller, dropping her shoulders.

"Girl, you have stepped into the land of possibilities, and you needed to shift your mindset about what was possible for you. If this is really what you want, then we need to take some time to prepare your mind, body, and soul, so that you can take action and build momentum toward the new life you'd like to live."

We took time to build an aligned action board, laying out all the steps from where she was to where she wanted to go, and we identified what was standing in her way. She desperately wanted to feel confident before having the conversation with Gerry. She wanted to feel ready and to say everything perfectly.

We then went into visualization and took time to imagine it was already a done deal. She thought back to previous times when she felt brave, proud, positive, and powerful to remind herself that she had what it takes inside and that she just needed to access these qualities again.

"How do you feel?" I asked.

"I feel hopeful and excited, and also a bit scared and skeptical," she said.

"That's normal," I reassured her.

Like most of us facing a BFC, Wilma needed to stop overthinking, embrace fear, and take action. She was in the process of unlocking her confidence by acting boldly and creating a new path to enjoy her journey.

Her eyes filled up with tears. "I just never feel ready to have the conversation."

I looked at her and smiled. "How would you know you are ready?"

She looked around before making eye contact with me. "I have no idea. I have been waiting to feel that way for five years."

"Here's the deal," I said as I leaned in closer to her. "You will never feel ready. Readiness does not exist. It's not a state of being but a feeling that comes after you take action."

Wilma's eyes widened.

"You can't feel ready to do something you've never done before. If you could have felt ready, you would have by now with all your preparation, overthinking, and strategizing," I said. "What I think you actually want to feel is brave enough to have the conversation and proud of yourself for taking care of your needs. In some ways, I think these things will make you feel like you got your power back and you can speak up again. Am I right?"

She nodded her head in agreement. "I have never thought of it like that."

I noticed how clear her voice was now and how confident she sounded. I looked her in the eye. "I know you are waiting to feel ready, but what you are really wanting is to feel confident."

She quickly looked away.

"You need to stop overthinking," I whispered. "Start embracing your fear."

She leaned in closer to me, eager to make change.

"Fear is just an indicator to move forward, not to hold you back."

She sighed out loud as if years of tension were melting from her shoulders.

"You will feel ready after you walk through the fear. You need to be willing to walk through the fear and experience how change transforms you when you take fear with you."

"Wait, what? What do you mean?" she asked.

I could tell she had not looked at fear from this perspective before. Most people don't. "Fear teaches us what we are made of and unlocks our confidence to a whole new level. Fear is a teacher that gives us the lesson on how to be proud, brave, positive, and powerful. Fear moves us into a better version of ourselves, a stronger and more confident version. Fear is our friend."

She wrinkled her forehead. "Umm..."

"Don't let fear dictate your life. Be intentional and design your life," I said. "It's go time."

She exhaled deeply. "Okay."

We reminisced about times she felt proud, brave, powerful, or positive, so that she could remember what that felt like and know that although she was waiting to feel confident, she had the necessary ingredients already. She needed to remind herself of this. We all do before we step out.

"Wilma, what do you want to feel after this conversation?" I asked.

"Well, I ideally want to feel certain that my conversation with Gerry will go well. I want to be brave and find my power again." A tear rolled down her cheek. "I want to feel proud of the work I do." I gently put my hands on her shoulders, looking at her as I nodded.

With a look of determination, Wilma picked up the phone and made the call to her boss. She stood up tall and she let him know that she was starting her own business and could take them on as her client, explaining her working terms and increased fee structure.

To her surprise, her boss didn't even flinch. He *knew* that she was valuable—her work spoke for itself and had saved his butt on many occasions—and he knew for sure that he didn't want to lose her. The real problem was that she had lost herself trying to mold herself to the expectations of her boss.

You will never feel ready. Readiness does not exist. It's not a state of being but a feeling that comes after you take action.

So right there and right then, he agreed to hire her company, paying her higher fees.

Everything changed in those five minutes of discomfort with her boss, which she had avoided for five years when she acted boldly and made the BFC that was buried down deep within herself. She found her voice again. No more contemplating, analyzing, overthinking, overpreparing, striving for perfection, or procrastinating out of fear. After she acted, she unlocked her confidence. She moved from employee to entrepreneur, and even more significantly, she went from feeling powerless to powerful. She became the boss of her own business and more importantly her life. She had found joy in her journey.

You are the CEO of your own life. You get to call the shots if you have the courage to embrace your fear and go after the life you want. No one can do this part for you, and nothing can give you this. No new relationship, job, or money will give you fulfillment. Your inner power will allow you to develop the skill of being aligned with your soul. This is how you find your voice and find your purpose.

In just under a year, her company took off. She stopped having anxiety attacks, learned to trust herself, tapped into her intuition, found her groove again, and got her evenings and weekends back. She even took a holiday to celebrate her first year in business, and boy, by the look of some pictures, she was radiating joy. She enjoyed her new life and the new version of herself she had created.

She started taking bigger risks and feeling brave; she expanded her business to new locations, feeling powerful; she hired more people, feeling proud; and she never once regretted that conversation that shifted her life, feeling positive. This is what a BFC did for her and can do for you if you have the courage to pursue it. Remember, it's courage, not confidence.

I saw her a few years later. She mentioned how she can't even imagine what her life would have been like if she never spoke up, if she never listened to her deep knowing, and if she never had the courage to face her fear. Wilma stepped out to step up and continues to build the habit of success and make the BFCs she needs.

She no longer waits to feel ready. Instead, she looks for opportunities to unlock her confidence and moves forward with courage. You can too. You've got this!

Why We Really Wait

As you know by now, when we say we are waiting to feel *ready*, what we are really saying is that we are waiting to feel *confident*. We want certainty, and we don't want to fail. But this is a catch-22 because confidence is the reward for making a decision and taking action. Confidence is developed through taking action and moving through fear. When we feel overwhelmed, emotions are hard to navigate, and we get stuck. We think we need to get unstuck first, because the model of confidence we know is backward. The real model of confidence starts with action: we develop our confidence, we feel ready, and finally we get unstuck. We get unstuck last. Most of us want to get unstuck before we take action, and so we stay waiting and never take action. But not you, because now you know the real model of confidence and you know the Get Unstuck, Cycle of Change Model.

Remember that we make decisions based on feelings. Dr. S. Colby Peters, founder and CEO of Human Systems, has created several tools to help improve mindfulness skills. In her Emotion Wheel II, she identifies eleven core human emotions and divides those into two categories: comfortable (accepted, interested, excited, loving, and confident) and uncomfortable (afraid, embarrassed, angry, sad, alone, and dislike). The wheel also identifies specific secondary emotions for each core emotion. And yes, all of us have all emotions.

The secondary emotions of confident are positive: proud, brave, and powerful. Isn't this what we are actually wanting to feel when we're about to make a big change? We want to feel positive about the outcome, proud that we have what it takes, brave enough to step out of our comfort zone, and powerful enough to overcome any challenges that arise. Confidence is what we have been waiting for all along, but it has been disguised as waiting to feel ready, which does not exist.

Waiting to feel ready is a protective mechanism, an excuse for not doing the work and stepping out. When you want more confidence, know that confidence comes after you take action. Not before. Never. You can be prepared but not confident so stop waiting for it.

The secondary emotions of afraid, on the uncomfortable side of the wheel, are stressed, overwhelmed, powerless, and anxious. These feelings describe the state of being stuck in life and how it feels to live in the fear, which we all experience before we make significant change. To cross over from uncomfortable to comfortable, you need to tap into your courage and take action. There is no other way to unlock your confidence. Let me say this again: in order to make change you need courage, not confidence. Oprah Winfrey defines courage as "feeling the fear and doing it anyway."

The Keys to Unlocking Your Confidence

Confidence isn't a destination; you won't wake up one day to find that you've arrived at this magical place. But I hope you can see that it can grow within you over time as you take steps forward with courage.

Author and motivational speaker Mel Robbins says that "confidence is embodied in action." Even when you're not feeling it in the moment, give yourself a little bit of grace and know you are well on your way when you take action. Confidence is about feeling comfortable with yourself, knowing you can trust yourself, and no longer comparing yourself to others. It's taking up space, being comfortable in your own skin, and celebrating your wins along the way. It's about stepping out of the wings and taking center stage to your life, the way you want it.

No matter how you feel right now, know that you can develop your confidence over time and tap into the emotional states of feeling positive, proud, powerful, and brave. The more chances you take, the more failures you have, and the more you learn about yourself. The further you go, the more confidence you develop. Confidence is the reward for taking action.

Before you go about making more BFCs in your life, I want you to know something important if you feel alone in your change. Standing out and being different as the first woman to do anything is not a reason to stand still. It may just mean you are a trailblazer or the only one who has the confidence to do it. As Jamie Kern Lima says, "You're not crazy, you're just first."

When you choose to be powerful, brave, positive, and proud, you inspire others to do the same. Think of all the women that we view as confident. None of them started that way; they all worked to get to that place and continue to do the daily work. It's how confidence works. You need to work your muscle daily. If you ask yourself, "Who am I to do this?" I would encourage you to respond, "Who am I *not* to do this?" and then do it anyway.

In an article published by Thrive Global, Aimee Stern writes, "Michelle Obama is the bravest of women on many levels mostly because she is willing to tell the world that she was not always brave." She had a nagging voice in her head, which we all have, telling her that she was "not smart enough, good enough, pretty enough, strong enough, mother enough—or brave enough—to be successful." She still stepped outside of her comfort zone to shine.

Lady Gaga, who rocks the stage and is powerful, brave, positive, and proud, did not start out that way and has insecurities that stand in her way. She shared with *Allure*, "I never felt beautiful, and I still have days that I don't feel beautiful… All of the insecurities that I've dealt with my whole life from being bullied when I was younger, they come right back up to bite me." Core scripts are real even for celebrities.

These women, and many other accomplished and iconic women, were not just born that way. They needed to discover their paths, and they're always works in progress, just like you and me. No one is perfect, no one has it all, but we are all more similar than we are different. We all have insecurities; some of us have worked on them more and worked through the fear.

If we want to feel empowered, as defined by *Merriam-Webster Dictionary*, we must live as "having the knowledge, confidence, means, or ability to do things or make decisions for oneself." There is no other way but to take action and stand out.

Take a look at Wonder Woman. William Moulton Marston, a Harvard-trained psychologist who believed in women's rights and brought women's empowerment to the forefront, created Wonder Woman as the first female superhero. She embodies the essence of empowerment, reminding us that true strength lies in embracing our unique qualities and channeling them into acts of courage.

Wonder Woman steps into courage. Her unwavering confidence is a shield against adversity and a source of inspiration. She is a reminder for all of us to embrace our boundless potential and our own strength and confidence. She is proud, brave, positive, and powerful, the full definition of confidence.

So remember: action leads to success. Take action. It's go time.

Taking Action Starts Now

As we reach the end of the book, let's take some action right now. Stand up and plant your feet hip distance apart, open your chest proudly, and stand in a Wonder Woman pose—one arm up reaching for new heights, with your other hand on your hip to feel grounded. As I like to say, head up and heart open.

Close your eyes and visualize yourself stepping into the next version of yourself. See her with admiration and excitement, and know that you are moving toward becoming the next version of yourself.

Speak positively about yourself by listing five qualities that affirm your potential:

I am...
I am...
I am...
I am...
I am...

Repeat your statements five times, each time saying them louder with more power and positivity. Let your ears hear it, your heart feel it, and your mind accept it.

Say them out loud to claim and unlock your confidence. Reflect back on the change you have made and complete these affirmations aloud:

I am proud of myself because...
I am brave because...
I am positive because...
I am powerful because...

Confidence Boosters

You have outgrown your current self and are upleveling. This is a good thing. You have stepped out of your *comfort zone*, into your *growth zone*, and you're about to enter the *possibility zone*. This is the most exciting phase to be in. There is no limit to who you can become or what you want to do. Everything is possible for you.

Here are some helpful tips to keep developing your confidence through the changes you will make in the future. We all need reminders and confidence boosters along the way. Try them out and see which are useful for you, and then take action and actually do them.

- **State How You Feel:** Call out your emotion, process it for ninety seconds, and ask what the emotion is teaching you.

- **Connect with Yourself:** Invest in yourself by asking yourself what you need.

- **Find Calmness:** Give yourself permission, and take some deep breaths.

- **Become Curious and Ask for Clarity:** What are you really scared of, and what do you truly desire? Explore your feelings for clarity.

- **Tap Into Your Courage:** Give yourself permission to be uncomfortable.

- **Be Open to Changes:** Ask yourself what else is possible.

- **Communicate Your Needs:** Set boundaries that honor who you are, your vision, and your values.

Fear moves us into
a better version of
ourselves, a stronger and
more confident version.
Fear is our friend.

- **Make a Commitment:** Keep your word to yourself and keep doing the work.

- **Focus on Being a Blessing and Contribute:** When you are setting goals, train your mind to focus on being a blessing to others, which will relieve stress.

- **Unlock Your Confidence:** Remind yourself how you have been proud, brave, positive, and powerful. Examples from the past and present will help you step into your future.

Ways to Love Yourself More

If we are unsure of the path ahead of us or feel a little lost, stuck, disconnected, or unfulfilled, that means our identity is changing. A great way to protect your confidence through change is to focus on loving yourself more by taking time to tend to your needs and desires. Here are some helpful ways to make yourself feel loved, which can be easy to implement. Remember you are moving through your fears toward love—this is a good thing.

- Have a morning routine—hand on heart affirmations, exercise, journaling.

- Declare your truth with "I am" statements.

- Remind yourself of the positives about yourself and your life by speaking affirmations in the morning and evening.

- Ask yourself empowering questions about how to have a great day and speak into possibility.

- Listen to your body, pay attention to your needs, and take care of yourself.

- Carve out time daily that is just for you, even if it's in moments or minutes.

- Appreciate, admire, respect, and love your body.

- Speak powerful words into your soul by saying "I am becoming."
- Find gratitude for the small things to program your mind to identify more opportunities for appreciation.
- Give yourself grace for mistakes, and know perfection does not exist.
- Forgive yourself for your mistakes and choose to let go and set yourself free.
- Forgive others and let things go to find more space for love.
- Take ownership for your life—all the good and bad, past and present—to become empowered for the future.
- Get excited to meet and embrace the next version of yourself.
- Always choose love, and you will never go wrong.

It's in Your Hands

Let's be real. At the end of the day, you don't need to do a single thing I've suggested in this book. You might decide not to update your mindset, embrace your fear, or plant seeds of possibility. You don't need to listen to your feelings or intuition for guidance, and you don't need to take time to invest in yourself. You have nothing to prove to anyone, including me and *especially* yourself. You are already worthy of all of the love, acceptance, and self-respect you could ever need. You are worthy now, as you have always been.

But that would mean you are settling—not living or rising to your potential—which will lead to regret. It's better to try and fail than to not try at all. There will always be people who are better than you in some area, but in reality you are only ever competing against the best version of yourself for yourself. That's it. That's all. No one can be better at being you than you. So be all of you.

It doesn't matter if someone else is prettier than you; there will *always* be someone prettier. It doesn't matter if someone else is smarter than you; there will *always* be someone smarter. It doesn't matter if someone else is more courageous, more loving, more energetic, gets more done, climbs higher heights, or gains more recognition. There will always be someone who seems to do more and be more. But you are on your own path, I am on my own path, and no two paths are the same.

The beauty is, when we stand next to each other, stripped down to our very essences, we are all the same. Unfinished, and yet already a masterpiece. A work in progress, and already enough. You came into this world with a spark that is uniquely yours, and nothing less than awe is appropriate when you are fully on display. As yourself, for yourself.

The Get Unstuck, Cycle of Change Model doesn't have the power to make you anything that you are not already. But it can help you discover, unlock, and amplify the secret power that is already there, a power that's been waiting patiently to be noticed and unleashed in your life. Your potential is waiting for you.

Every step in this process helps to remove your block to access that power, and the process results in greater confidence. Which helps remove more blocks. Which results in greater confidence. That's why it's called a cycle. The Get Unstuck, Cycle of Change Model will help you step into your brilliance because you were born for greatness. When you step into your brilliance, you become a gift back to the world as you inspire others to do the same. This is where change is possible in the world, where we narrow the gap between genders, and we all rise together for not only ourselves but for each other.

If you stick with it, big, beautiful, and positive changes will start to flow more naturally for you. In time, you will be able to look back and say, "How on earth did I get from *there* to *here*?!" Let me give you a hint: it's because you had the courage to make a BFC!

The reason I'm most excited for you to make your BFC is the impact that you will have on the women and young girls around you. In a world that's always trying to get us to play just a little bit smaller, we need as many examples as we can get of women playing a bit bigger. We need more women to start businesses, enter industries that are male-dominated, do work they're passionate about, give to their communities, share their ideas, take bigger risks, and confidently expect full value in return for the value they share. We need more women who aren't afraid to step out of relationships that are not serving them and who choose to take better care of themselves. We need more women to take chances on themselves because they know they are worth it. We need more women to feel that they can work and raise a family and don't need to choose. We need all of us to play full out and to have less fear, less guilt, and more joy, so we can reach new heights. Together. One step at a time. Step by step. Stepping forward. Will you do this?

Because when you rise, we rise. And when we rise, they rise too. There is room for all of us to shine; it's not a competition. When we step into our greatness, we can help others find theirs. I believe this is what life is all about: becoming who we are meant to be and helping others see their potential in the process. This is what I want for my daughter, Claire; this is what I want for all the little girls who enter my dance studio; this is what I want for every woman in the world that feels stuck, for every person who wants to make change. It's time for us to step out to step up and make the change in the world.

So even if you don't feel ready, please just take just one step in the direction of the change you want to see in your life. Because that is one step toward the change we want to see in the world. And we need you now, more than ever before. When you become more of who you are meant to be, it will inspire others to do the same.

To the masterpiece you already are, and to the masterpiece that you are becoming: you are beautifully unfinished. Find your voice. Embrace yourself and make that BFC. Turn that page and write a new chapter of your life that serves you. After all, we are just like books: most people judge us only by our covers, some skim the introduction, some are critics full of judgment, and few truly appreciate our value and depth of inner knowledge. But all of our chapters together make us magnificent and the greatest love story ever written. The story of self-love. The story of confident women going after their dreams, because they had the courage to pursue Big Freakin' Change.

Hand on Heart

Let's do some affirmations. Repeat the following statements out loud, and let them land in your heart to plant a seed of possibility that awakens your brilliance.

I choose to let go of things that are no longer serving me.

I embrace myself for all that I am today.

I will listen to my mind, body, and soul, and I will connect to my highest potential and my highest self.

I am brave, proud, positive, and powerful. I am confident. I am beautifully unfinished.

I trust myself and give myself permission to step into the next version of myself.

Close your eyes, place your hand on your heart, and ask yourself these questions:

What is really standing in the way of my BFC?

What do I need to let go of to fully step into the next version of myself?

How can I remove my obstacles?

How can I trust myself more?

How can I love myself more?

P.S. You may be scared of not reaching your potential or of living with regret, but when you are true to yourself, you can't go wrong. Anything and everything becomes possible.

10
STEPPING INTO GREATNESS

"A journey of a thousand miles begins with a single step."

LAO TZU

WHEN I WAS twenty years old in my second year of university, I had the opportunity to go backpacking through South America with one of my closest friends, Jen, over spring break. We had always bonded at parties over good food, fits of laughter, fun fashion, and a deep sense of adventure, all of which were on the agenda for this trip.

Although there was so much we hoped to see and do, we were most excited to hike the Inca Trail and take in the gorgeous beauty of Machu Picchu, the five-hundred-year-old ruins known as the Lost City of the Incas.

Not for the faint of heart, it's a five-day twenty-six-mile hike through the Andes, with an average daily elevation gain of one thousand meters. When we arrived in Peru, we booked the hike with a local guide company and prepared ourselves for the journey. We were both in decent shape and worked out on the treadmill with an incline, naively thinking that gave us a sense of what the big hike would feel like. We were feeling pretty prepared and physically ready.

The day before our departure, we met our tour operator and our fellow travelers at a tiny Peruvian café and were given instructions for the next day. "Arrive at 6 a.m. sharp," the tan-skinned long-blond-haired American agent said. "Bring all your gear packed and ready to go. You're about to go on the adventure of a lifetime." We signed the waivers without a glance at what they said, feeling an abundance of optimism and *beaming* with anticipation for the next day's adventure.

That night we slept well and arrived extra early in the morning. Carrying our brand-new backpacks overflowing with gear, our excitement blinded us to the sheer weight we'd be carrying for the next five days. As we waited for everyone else to arrive, I recalled all that I had read about Machu Picchu. I pictured in vivid detail the aerial photographs of the stunning citadel in the center of mountain peaks. It was breathtaking. It felt magical and surreal.

Something about this journey called out to my heart and extended an invitation and a promise that I couldn't quite articulate, but I knew I wanted to accept. Maybe you have had a calling or invitation in your heart, a sense of knowing which adventures or challenges you need to face or want to explore. I pondered what might be in store for me, and for the first time since planning this trip, I noticed fear creeping in.

"I can do this! Right?" I thought, trying to push the fear out of view. "I *can* do this! I'm fit, I'm young, I'm brave. I can *do* this!"

Whenever we do anything new, we often brush up against both fear *and* excitement. As we've learned earlier, it's the same physiological experience in the body interpreted differently in our minds. I did not know that at the time, but I certainly know it now and tell everyone I can, because it's profound.

Once the rest of the group was assembled, a handsome athletic bushy-bearded young Peruvian man walked toward us with a big smile and greeted us with a thick Spanish accent. "Hello, my name is Johnny, and I will be your tour guide on this adventure." He took a moment and looked at each one of us intently. He seemed to be assessing if we had what it took to complete the trek, giving us each an approving nod before moving on to the next. It was as if he was looking at my soul and knew something I didn't. Sometimes our guides in life have a knowledge and perspective we have yet to discover.

I was pretty sure his name wasn't *actually* Johnny. Most local people working in the tourism industry choose an English name to make it easier for us tourists. I made a mental note to ask him his Peruvian name on our trip.

"We will stick together," Johnny said, "and everything will be okay. Okay? Vamos!" His confidence and friendly presence made it easy to like and trust him. He was fit, charismatic, organized, and had a spark in his eyes. As an experienced tour guide, Johnny would not just guide us to Machu Picchu but also keep us safe along the way. I was glad to feel that sense of trust in him so instinctively and quickly. And if I'm totally honest, the fact that he was muy guapo (very handsome) didn't hurt either!

We hopped in an old beat-up white van that looked like it had hiked the trail itself a few thousand times. We drove for an hour along winding dirt trails and bumpy cobblestone roads to the trailhead. Driving through the final little village, I was taken by the explosion of color all around us. The Peruvian women were stunning in vibrant multicolored dresses, with gorgeous brown eyes and big smiles that seemed just for us. Their long braids draped down the sides of their bodies, swaying back and forth as they balanced large wicker baskets of puffed quinoa on their heads. Though I was taking in the visual beauty of the scene, the invisible beauty of their spirits is what struck me most. I sensed a quiet strength within them that I instinctively admired. It was almost as if they had a sense of peace and knowing and lived within a land of possibilities. The whisper of the invitation I had felt was making itself known once again; maybe I could experience this quiet strength too. Whether it was a sense of knowing or my intuition calling, I felt something magical. It was a force of flow, something far bigger than me. One moment was ending, and another was about to begin. I felt alive, protected, and inspired.

The van jolted to an abrupt stop, and Johnny hopped out to slide the dented door open for us. "Your adventure awaits!" The bright sun shone warmly on our faces, the fresh mountain air a perfect complement. We filed out of the stuffy van and geared up, clicking our backpack waist belts one at a time, as if we were fastening our seat belts for the ride of a lifetime.

All together we were a group of twelve hikers plus Johnny. We had flown in from all over the world for this experience: Australia, Brazil, Italy, the United States, Korea, and Canada. The diversity of our homelands was matched by the diversity of our ages, careers, and life experiences. On the surface, we had very little common ground, but the anticipation of the shared experience on the Inca Trail quickly bonded us.

I found my place directly behind Johnny on the trail. I noticed every new and beautiful detail around me. Blooming trees were nestled in pockets of ancient ruins and covered in bright green moss. Jen and I were speechless, taking it all in. Lost in the splendor surrounding us, I found the first few hours much easier than I expected. I felt confident that I was capable. The only challenge was acclimatizing to the lower oxygen levels of the higher elevation.

"We will get to almost fourteen thousand feet above sea level," Johnny informed us. "So the higher we go, be prepared to take deep breaths as the oxygen level decreases." It was like anything in life: the higher we climb, the more intentional we need to become.

I noticed then that I was feeling a little bit lightheaded, and I took Johnny's advice, inhaling and exhaling slowly with intention. "In through my nose and out through my mouth," I repeated to myself.

"*Breathe*, Cara. Remember to *breathe*!" I said to myself in between slow and deep breaths. Yes, my body would breathe automatically, but I needed to do it with intention to sustain the challenge ahead.

I used the opportunity to remind myself to be proactive: not only breathing deeper, but eating snacks regularly to maintain my energy, staying hydrated, and pacing myself with the entire journey in mind. I had to be intentional with my steps, my breath, and my energy. It wasn't about walking side by side with Jen anymore; it was about listening to my body and trusting my inner guide. We were all doing it together collectively, while maintaining integrity individually. I knew I could not compare my trek to anyone else's if I wanted to make it to the top.

The first day's hike was long, but one of the easier days in terms of the increase in elevation. We arrived at our campsite just as golden hour set in, our backs sore and our legs feeling like jelly. To our delight and major relief, tents had already been pitched for us, and a feast prepared and waiting under a white plastic tarp strung to nearby trees. Jen and I were not handy or outdoorsy at all, so the fact that all this had been done for us felt like Christmas.

Eating every last bite of our portions, we sat together as a group, told stories, recounted the day's journey, and enjoyed the kind of laughter that only comes with exhaustion earned in pursuit of a

It was a force of flow, something far bigger than me. One moment was ending, and another was about to begin.

worthy goal. The first day complete, I already felt as if I had accomplished something big, and it seemed my trail mates felt the same. I felt I was on a path of discovery, not only to see the land but to explore who I was becoming.

Maybe you are on a path now too, feeling open to discovery and pushing your limits, developing a new sense of confidence on your journey of challenge and change.

Jen and I went back to our tent and prepared for bed. Unlacing and removing our boots, we weren't even remotely prepared for the nasty smell that sprung up to meet us, filling our tent with a reminder of the day's effort. We looked at each other, burst out laughing, and reached in unison for the tent zipper to let in some fresh air.

I couldn't believe how bad we smelled! No perfume or hot showers for these city slickers. We fancied ourselves to be quite fashionable and sophisticated ladies, but the smell combined with our considerably unfashionable attire plus the dirt on our hands and faces painted a very different image.

"Who even *are* we?" I asked her, rubbing some lamb's wool on my newly formed blisters, which were worse than any blister from dance that I'd ever had.

She smiled. "We are *adventurers*, Cara, and we can do anything!"

I already considered myself quite adventurous from my previous trips backpacking around Europe and moving to foreign countries by myself, but it felt even more true that day.

We finished changing for bed, removing our sweaty, stinky clothes and replacing them with dry wool long johns and shirts. We nuzzled ourselves in our sleeping bags, trying to find comfort on the hard rocky ground. The sense of accomplishment, increased confidence, and sheer exhaustion from the day proved a potent sleep medicine.

The next two days felt mostly like an extension of the first one. We woke up with the sun shining, ate a hearty breakfast, and hiked up and down steep mountain passes for most of the daylight hours. We arrived at a campsite with food prepared for us and miraculously timed to be hot and ready upon our arrival. Each day ended with an early bedtime to give us the rest we needed for the next day. The difference between the first day and the third was most obvious in the increased soreness of our legs and backs, and the speed in which exhaustion set in during the day's hike. We were well on our way, and I started to become determined to get there faster, growing more eager and less patient. We were pushing our physical limits, and you could see it in our gait. What had started as a bounce in each step was more like a drag in each step.

The mental aspect of the hike was on display as well. On day one, I would scan the horizon to find a distinctive landmark off in the distance and use it as a goal to motivate me to keep moving forward. But as we started our trek on day four, the landmarks I used for motivation had become noticeably closer and more frequent—closer to one hundred meters away than one thousand. On the steepest climbs, the distance shrunk down to the space between one step and the next. I felt the burn with each step I took.

Apparently sensing what was on my mind, Johnny turned around, looked me in the eyes, and waved his arms in a circular motion from sky to ground. "You are doing *great*, Cara! One step at a time, okay?" He knew I needed that motivation at that exact time, or I might have stopped.

"Just.

one.

step.

at.

a.

time.

That's all it takes!"

As if wanting to get in on the encouragement, the clouds above gifted us with a cooling sprinkling of rain. I received each drop with gratitude as it hit my neck and dripped down the back of my shirt.

Hearing Johnny singing softly to himself, almost in a chant, I wondered if he had magical powers that he had been saving up for this exact moment of rain. The Korean couple behind me giggled in apparent agreement.

Drip.

Drip. Drip.

Drip. Drip. Drizzle. Drizzle. Woosh.

Within seconds, the light sprinkling that provided relief from the heat of our exertion transformed itself into a proper Peruvian downpour. We scrambled to preserve whatever dryness we could by whipping out our rain ponchos and covering ourselves.

We were already exhausted and now soaking wet as well. "I didn't sign up for this shit," I thought. "What the heck was I thinking, and who the hell did I think I was to be able to do this hike?" My confidence fell away as the rain poured down.

Over the next fifteen minutes, the clouds darkened the sky so that it appeared to be on the cusp of nightfall; the raindrops got bigger and faster, drenching us. I squinted my eyes, trying to provide protection from the downpour, and I was nervous with every step I took. Our path was no longer visible as factors outside our control took over.

As we began a new descent, Johnny turned around again with a new sense of urgency. I could see it in his eyes and instantly got scared; I could see that our guide was scared too. "We need to keep moving, please. Don't let the rain slow you down. One step at a time. Keep moving."

Crack! Boom!

I didn't see the lightning, but it was so close that it felt as if it was coming from inside me. My heart skipped a beat, and my stomach flipped. "Holy shit!" I screamed and leaped off the ground.

Despite the mud that was now forming under our feet, Johnny had picked up the pace and expected us to do the same. I started to jog for fear of being left behind.

The forecast had called for clear skies every step of the way, but Mother Nature had other plans, as she so often does. All we could do was trust Johnny and keep moving forward.

"Are we going to be okay, Johnny?" Gustavo, the Brazilian, shouted above the pouring rain and thunder in the sky. "Is this rain going to last?"

Johnny looked back at us with an awkward forced smile, ignored the question, and instead replied, "We need to keep going, and quickly please. Once the sun goes down, we won't be able to see our path. Follow me. Please." If we didn't follow his directions, we would be lost in the dark.

When our plans change, we can often feel lost in the dark and need a guide to help us.

Two hours passed with no respite from the storm. We began to see a trickle of other hikers heading back the way we had come toward camps; a few of them were even being carried on the backs of their guides. I couldn't help but feel grateful that wasn't me, and then the next second, I wished it *was* me. I flip-flopped from fear to courage in the moments of challenge.

I had started this hike with the confidence that I could complete it, even if it took every ounce of my energy and determination. But as my feet slipped in the mud, and my body shivered from the cold rain that had found its way onto every inch of my skin, I began to really doubt that I had it in me for the first time.

"What the hell was I thinking? I'm just a city girl. I'm not cut out for this shit!" I thought. "Why did I think I had this in me? I'm a dancer, not a hiker!"

My self-doubt and discouraging thoughts quickly found the path of least resistance to fear, and I felt it taking over with every slippery step I took. I instantly blamed myself for the mess I was in, when clearly the storm was beyond my control. Physically, I was exhausted but managed to push through. The real battleground was no longer the mud underneath me or the rain pouring down on me but within my mind. I hadn't even considered my mindset going into the hike, and now that lack of preparation was becoming evident. I had never been in this situation before and had no idea how to navigate it. I felt helpless, stressed, lost, and definitely stuck.

I was clearly not alone.

"Are you sure we should keep going?" Suzie, the Australian doctor, yelled out to Johnny. "Is it *safe* to keep going? It's been three hours, and it's just getting worse out here. Should we turn around?"

"Just keep moving forward, everyone. Trust me, please. We need to keep moving forward. Watch your step and move *quickly*. Vamos!"

Mustering extra energy over a less muddy patch of trail, I ran ahead to be directly beside Johnny, hoping to borrow some of his courage to replace what I'd lost.

"This is getting intense, hey?" I said, looking in his eyes and hoping for some encouragement. Dusting off my Spanish, I asked him, "Es tu nombre Johnny, la verdad?" (Is your name actually Johnny?)

He smiled at the personal question in his mother tongue and responded, "No, me nombre es Javier Jesus, pero es difícil para turistas." (No, my name is Javier Jesus, but it's difficult for the tourists.)

"Gracias por todo," I replied with genuine gratitude. (Thank you for everything.) I wanted him to know that I appreciated him. And to be honest, I also wanted him to be as invested as possible in our safety and I wanted to know what was going on.

Without warning, a massive branch of lightning filled the sky in front of us and struck the ground. The thunder was unlike any I'd heard before, like a wave of explosions pouring into the valley and bouncing from mountain to mountain with us in the middle. I screamed and instinctively grabbed for Johnny's arm. I wasn't sure I could go on. Fear rushed through me like I had never experienced before. I felt numb. Frozen and stuck. My legs were heavy and I couldn't move.

He pushed me forward to keep moving. Matching my steps to Johnny's, I found some comfort in our shared rhythm, and repeated to myself with each step, "Keep going, Cara. One more step." That internal voice became a mantra with each step. My perception of time blurred, carrying me forward through the singular purpose of simply taking the next step, one step at a time, even when I needed support to keep moving forward.

The storm didn't worsen, but it stayed with us for our entire journey that day. We pressed forward, trusting our guide, and using his faith in us to find our faith in ourselves.

It took four more hours to reach our final camp; it had felt impossible, given the challenges, to reach it but somehow we made it. In that time, we passed at least thirty hikers retracing their steps toward their perception of safety, each one's face a mixture of disappointment and fear.

I felt pride swell up within me that no one from our group was among that number; the warmth of that emotion momentarily made me forget the shiver present in my body. We had made the decision to move forward, despite the challenge, discomfort, and uncertainty.

We didn't know how our journey would turn out, but we continued to take the next step.

A Plan Needs to Pivot

The moment we stepped into our camp that night and sat down by the prepared fire, protected by yet another white tarp hung between the trees, tears started running down my face uncontrollably, camouflaged only by the drips from my soaking hair.

A few tears were shed in relief at making it to camp safely, a few more to acknowledge and release the fear that had been a constant companion that day. A few more still seemed to be an expression of joy I couldn't explain. I made it. I was going to be okay. I was safe, and it was worth it.

Huddling around the fire, our little tribe of hikers sat in silence, letting the flicker of the fire and the drumming of the rain on the tarp do the talking. This fire felt warmer and more comforting than usual, as we individually and together processed what we had just experienced. We sat closer together than we had on other nights, as if in acknowledgment of the bond we shared having gone through fear together.

Our hosts at this camp had prepared a freshly cooked meal of guinea pig and rice, a meal I never would have tried in any other circumstance.

"Hmmm," I thought, "I guess I'm someone who eats guinea pig now! I'm a guinea pig eater!" I laughed out loud at myself with the group. It felt weird and wrong because I had had a pet guinea pig, Sandy, as a child.

But I was no longer a child. I was a woman. I could change who I was and what I could do. I could give myself permission to change into who I would become. I was here on a mountain in the middle of nowhere with a group of mostly strangers that had transformed into a band of brave warriors. I chuckled quietly at this new little piece of my identity and wondered what else had changed in me that day that I hadn't yet noticed.

When the storm had begun, I didn't feel that I had what it took to keep moving forward. I didn't feel *ready* for the challenge. But every step I took told a different story. It wasn't a feeling of readiness that moved me forward, but the movement forward that showed me I had been ready all along. For seven hours, we had hiked through the fiercest storm I had ever experienced, slipping on muddy paths up and down steep mountains, all while soaked to the bone and shivering to the core.

How *exactly* do you get ready for that?

How do you prepare for the unknown in any journey, feeling completely ready for whatever outcome awaits you? You can only prepare so much for the challenge you are facing and the BFC you are making. Even with a plan in place, you may need to pivot to make your necessary BFC.

By focusing on the smallest possible increment of the goal of making it to safety—one step—our whole group had managed to keep moving forward. We did it one step at a time.

I've always been quite competitive, which is probably part of why I spent the majority of the trek positioned directly behind Johnny. Jen liked being in the back, and I liked being in the front. Maybe I thought that being close to Johnny would convince me that I belonged or encourage me when I was defeated. Whatever the reason, I couldn't find the strength alone.

My biggest competitor that day was not anyone else in the group but the version of myself who'd started the journey a few days before. She was strong, fit, and determined to complete the difficult hike to Machu Picchu.

Yet she was no match for the version of me I had found in the midst of the storm. My transformation came in a different package than I expected, but it was the gift I didn't know I needed. Through that experience, I stepped up (and sometimes tripped) into the next version of myself and could feel it in my mind, body, and soul, one step at a time.

I learned a valuable lesson: the path into *what could be* begins with the acceptance of *what already is*. To move forward with each new step, I had to accept the reality of the one I was already in.

Our paths rarely follow our plans, hopes, or desires, but we can often find a better one if we learn to collaborate with our reality, instead of wishing it was different. The path through the storm was surrender, which is not the same thing as giving up. When we surrender to what is, we find a firmer footing to create what could be. Instead of falling apart, we often find ourselves falling forward, falling upward, and falling into the next step of achieving our dreams. I invite you to do the same when you face storms in your own life.

Sometimes you have to let go of your expectations, dreams, and wishes and accept what is and go through a challenging storm to reach new heights. Occasionally you have no great option and you lose something no matter what you choose. But in time, you will gain too. You just don't know it when it's happening. Through a storm comes strength. And with strength, you learn to trust yourself, which is the greatest gift of all.

In just seven hours, from mountain peak to mountain peak, minute to minute, and step by step, I had transformed. I had changed from someone who could complete a challenging hike to someone who could complete a challenging hike in the midst of one of the fiercest storms! I watched my own nature rise to meet the challenge, and my confidence grew in the process.

I wasn't just a hiker anymore. I was now a *storm hiker*. I looked around the fire, aware of the change I felt within me and acknowledging the change that I assumed everyone else was experiencing too. It was impossible to be pushed this hard for this long and not experience one of the gifts that challenge offers. Challenge changes us. This felt like the reason I was supposed to be on the hike. The invitation I had felt.

As I took my last sip of tea and went to my tent, I wondered what tomorrow would bring. Would the storm continue, or would we get to hike in the warmth of the sun again? Although I still preferred the latter, as a newly defined storm hiker, the prospect of hiking through a storm again somehow seemed a little less daunting. I knew I could do it, and I felt ready to walk through the storm. Even if the circumstances didn't change one bit, I had and so had my perspective. I fell asleep, reflecting on this new truth and new identity, and drifted into

When our plans change, we can often feel lost in the dark and need a guide to help us.

what was the best sleep of my entire life. My body fully rested while my heart released. My mind was at ease, and my sense of wonder expanded. I could face challenges and be changed through the storms in life. This is the same for you and for all of us.

Far too often, we only see other people's end points and not their starting points or detours, so we make assumptions about them. We can feel as though we don't measure up. Truth is we just don't talk about the challenges, twists, turns, and changes we all make along the way. We have no idea the storms others have experienced in their lives to reach their peaks.

Renewed Gratitude

The next morning, I woke up to the noticeable absence of pounding rain. The warm sun glowed over a nearby mountain, extending an invitation to complete our journey and see the majesty of Machu Picchu. I was aware that we wouldn't have this opportunity if we'd turned around yesterday. I had a renewed gratitude for Johnny—Javier Jesus—for his expert guidance the day before. I was grateful that he believed in our capability to make it through the storm. He saw something in us that we did not. It wasn't only mountain and hiking experience that he cared about, but our internal awareness and sense of self too.

Over breakfast, I asked him how often he hikes through storms like that with groups. "Oh, Carita," he said with a gentle smile, "that was the first time. Usually I would turn back. But when I looked at all of you, I knew in my heart that you could make it. I just felt it. You just needed a little push. And I was right, wasn't I?"

My eyes widened. He saw potential in me? How could he have known that the city-girl dancer with a high ponytail and brand-new hiking boots and backpack had what it takes?

"How did you know?" I asked.

"You have courage," he said as he looked at me. "You have courage and confidence, and with those, you can do anything."

My eyes filled with tears because at one point, I felt I had lost my courage and confidence altogether in the storm. It was almost as if the more steps I took, the worse and more fearful I felt. Until I made it. And then a new sense of myself was created.

He gently put his hand on my head as if he was blessing me. "When you have courage and confidence, they never leave you," he said.

I took a moment to let that sink in with me. It was a divine moment that I will always cherish.

"Even when you don't feel confident or you lose your confidence, it's still there underneath, at your core," I thought to myself. He had a message that I needed to receive. This was why I'd been called to the hike. Not just to see the beautiful landscape but to discover this beautiful gift of self-awareness and what I was capable of.

With full bellies and a caffeine boost, we set out on the trail again, one last time. It was day five and our fearless guide announced to us that the hardest part was behind us. We were only three hours away from the destination for which we had set out four days ago. We had come so far already, but it felt like time passed more slowly as our anticipation increased and we approached our destination.

Although my blisters were still raw, I didn't mind them too much. I knew that if I could handle hiking seven hours through a crazy storm in the middle of the Andes, I could handle some sores on my feet and some storms in life. Jen and I were walking side by side celebrating how far we came.

My backpack somehow felt lighter that day, even though all my gear was packed and accounted for, including a bunch of wet clothes. I wasn't focused on the weight I was carrying but the strength I had gained. My perspective changed because I changed.

My capacity for carrying myself through this intense experience had increased since yesterday. I joked with Jen that I could probably strap her on my back and carry her if needed. We both knew we would just fall to the ground, laughing, and probably pee ourselves trying to get up. The storm had been temporary but the capacity it gave me was propelling me forward with strength that would be permanent.

It felt like my capacity to carry *everything* had increased. I had been pushed to my limit and then some. My capacity expanded, and

I felt a new sense of strength from within. Every step I took that day felt like an incremental arrival into a new version of myself. A version of myself who knew she was capable of taking bigger risks and achieving greater things by taking bolder steps. A new version of myself who stood a little taller and reached a little further. A new version of myself who knew how to dream something into being. A new version of myself who felt more courageous.

I hadn't even made it to Machu Picchu yet, and I already caught myself dreaming about my next adventure. "What else do I want to do? How will I challenge myself next? What changes do I need to make in my life when I get home?"

Do you find yourself thinking about the next great thing you can do, before you've even finished the BFC you're doing now?

I used to believe dreaming was a problem, but now I think it's a gift. It helps us become expansive and enter the land of possibilities. We discover what we are truly capable of.

After two and a half hours, we neared a mountain peak and rounded the top for the final stretch. It was the culmination of all our planning, training, and hiking. I was prepared for the final steps, but nothing could have prepared us for the view that greeted us from the peak.

In an instant, every picture I had admired in anticipation of this moment felt like it didn't do justice to the reality before me. My jaw dropped in admiration. I saw the majesty of ancient architecture suspended in the arms of nature and the majesty of the human spirit expressed through the creativity and hard work necessary to build something this grand. How awe-inspiring it was for this place from long ago to remind us of what we are capable of. I felt God's presence and the universe's energy give me a warm embrace. A divine voice whispered to me, "There are no limits for you, my dear. You were born for greatness." I looked up to the sky and reached my arms up in appreciation as if I was thanking God himself. I looked around, thanking the universe for supporting me. I looked down at my muddy hiking boots and thanked myself for taking the steps.

"Wow."

"Holy shit, Cara! We *did* it," Jen squealed as she hugged me tight. We bounced around in a circle like little schoolgirls doing a happy dance as we laughed with pride, relief, delight, and joy. We had so much joy. We found joy in the journey even though we came through a storm.

There's something profound about pausing to celebrate a moment of victory: it reminds our future selves of everything we're capable of and contributes to an ongoing habit of success. I let the sun warm my body and brighten my soul as I felt it expand.

The final trek brought us into the ruins where we could admire the Incan skill and artistry up close. Each rock was stacked perfectly. Carvings depicting ancient Inca life pulled us into the stories that were still depicted on the walls.

The reward of seeing Machu Picchu both from the nearby mountain and up close in detail was worth every labored step of love. The journey itself had proven to be its own reward. In that, I made a vow to never despise whatever journey I happened to be in the middle of; I would instead ask it to reveal its reward to me afterward. We had the view of a lifetime, joy that filled our hearts, and the capability to unlock a new, deep sense of confidence. These were the gifts that fear offered us. These were the gifts that facing a challenge gave us, and it will give them to you too.

After a couple of hours of exploration, we were ready to return. Our little group congregated in a circle and hugged each other tightly. We locked eyes with each other as if sharing the greatest farewell blessings we could offer. I couldn't even remember what had made us feel so different from each other just five days ago. We were all the same now.

I spotted Javier Jesus smiling at us from a distance. I walked over to him and gave him a tight hug with every ounce of gratitude I had within me. "Gracias por todo, Javier Jesus!" (Thank you for everything, Javier Jesus!)

Switching to English, I said, "I don't know how to thank you for the journey you took us on these last five days. But I want to try. Thank you for seeing the path when we couldn't, and thank you for believing in us. You are the best guide. I will always remember you."

He seemed moved by my words.

I put my hands on his shoulders and looked intently into his eyes. "I want you to know that I see you and appreciate the gift you gave us on this journey. Without your guidance, we wouldn't have known the way. Without your wisdom, we wouldn't have known how to stay on the path. And without your faith in us during the storm, we wouldn't have found it within ourselves. Muchas gracias por todo.

"Machu Picchu is pretty awesome too!" I winked at him and playfully punched his shoulder in farewell.

He looked at me intently. In that moment, I had a flashback to the beginning of the trip when he looked at each one of us in this way. It felt like he'd been assessing us for something. I knew now that that something was courage.

Life's experiences and challenges give us courage beyond measure. Fear brings courage to the center stage of life. Fear opens many doors, especially the one we have kept closed in avoidance. Fear offers gifts that provide us with self-awareness beyond what we could ever have imagined. This is how we become more of ourselves. It's through fear, challenges, and storms of life that our next versions are revealed. We grow the most not through victory, but through storms.

There is no shortcut, no detour, and certainly no easy answer. You have to go *through* it. It may not happen how we imagined, or in the time frame we want, but this process *always* provides us the opportunity to become more of who we are. It's the silver lining that accompanies us if we are willing to focus on *being* and staying the course in the storms of life. Always. Every. single. time. Step. by. step.

Every decision we make and every step we take changes us ever so slightly. When we direct those steps with intention toward a Big Freakin' Change and use the Get Unstuck, Cycle of Change Model as our compass, we discover that the biggest change is always the one that happens *within* us. These types of change happen *for* us, not *to* us. The inside work is always our responsibility and offers us our greatest opportunities to advance to the next version of ourselves.

It was on this trip to Machu Picchu that I learned that sometimes you need a guide to show you the way, reveal your potential, and encourage you. Such a guide is especially important when you feel lost, stuck, overwhelmed, or scared. Sometimes you are not meant to do it alone. We are all wired for connection. We need connection, and we deserve connection. We cannot connect to others until we connect with ourselves—our insecurities, hopes, dreams, and desires. This is how transformation happens.

You can't prepare for every storm. But you need to go through them by trusting yourself and your intuition. Continue taking steps forward, and embrace the invitation that is waiting for you on the other side of fear. It's okay to take action when you don't feel ready. Readiness is not a state of being but a feeling that comes after you take action.

Pay attention to your own needs first. Don't let the criticism or opinions of others dictate whether or not you move forward, or how you take each step. No one has walked your path, and no one knows where you want to go but you. Your goal should never be to satisfy your critics. And trust me, when you're trying to do something extraordinary in your life, you will have plenty of them. But the people who are also doing extraordinary things will understand you and celebrate you. You will inspire others who also have courage, and you may bring up insecurities in those who lack courage. But do it anyway. Do it for yourself; do it for others to inspire them to step into their greatness too.

True integrity is never about aligning with someone else's expectations; it's about aligning with your own. That's where peace is found in the midst of any challenge, change, or storm.

It was on the hike that I truly understood we are all on our personal paths and the only person we need to compete with is the best version of ourselves. We cannot compare our journey with anyone else's for it's *only* ours to experience. We all find our ways at different times and through different storms when we are called to make a BFC. When we focus on where our feet are planted and the path we climb, we become powerful and step into greatness—our greatness. You will become powerful. Don't be alarmed that as you climb higher and reach new peaks, fewer people will surround you. This is just a normal part of the process.

When you reach those mountain peaks or new peaks in life, you suddenly understand the infinite possibilities that await you. The seed of possibility that you planted has grown into your present reality, and a new seed of possibility is now available for you to plant. What will you do with it? What is possible for you now that wasn't before? Your viewpoint changes as your mind expands and your potential increases.

Big Freakin' Changes have a way of updating our perspectives on life, awakening us to new possibilities, and shifting our identity. Don't be surprised if you get to the peak of that change and find yourself with a new hunger for change in another area of your life, a new dream you never considered before. If you have ever worked really hard to accomplish or experience something and then asked yourself, "Is this it for me?" that's an indication you have simply reached a new peak. Now you get to choose to stay there and take it all in or begin another climb. There are benefits to both. When you reach the peaks, you unlock new potential not only in what you can do but also in who you can become in the process.

Perspectives gleaned from the highs and lows, twists and turns, challenges and changes are what brings us to the next version of ourselves. At times, it can be easy to look to our past with judgment, guilt, and possibly regret and rely only on hope to guide us forward into the future.

Remember, as Vivian Greene wrote: "Life isn't about waiting for the storm to pass... It's about learning how to dance in the rain." And sister, I so hope you dance. I hope you bust a freakin' move! A big freakin' move.

When the rain stops, and it will, there will be new beginnings awaiting. Sometimes you need to walk in the rain and in the darkness and accept that's part of the process. You will be uncomfortable and fearful at times, which will make you question your abilities and decisions. Choosing not to move when you are stuck is making a choice too. Staying in limbo causes you stress. Hoping for change without taking action costs you your peace. It's time to keep climbing, keep dancing, and soon you will find your groove.

Sometimes the sun will shine and other times the rain will pour, but at all times there are opportunities for gratitude and growth. You will learn to appreciate it all. Your next version of yourself is emerging.

Open your eyes to see her and embrace her. Let her in, and let go of people, things, and situations that belong to past versions of yourself. You are meant to change and evolve—this is why we are here. You are no longer stuck: you have the tools to navigate change, and you have found your courage that will lead you to your confidence. You don't need to wait to feel ready.

You may have already made one change and are on to the next, or maybe you are reevaluating the change you wanted to make. Either way... your timing is *perfect*. This is your cue to step out and take center stage in your own life. No more waiting in the wings, hoping for things to change. Make the change. Take the step. You were meant to change. Enjoy your BFC. It's time to step out because your life is waiting for you.

Place your hand on your heart. Take a deep breath and remember you've got this.

To making your BFC that changes you in the process,

P.S. I hope you dance.

ACKNOWLEDGMENTS

To all the remarkable girls and women yearning for transformation but unsure of where to start, this book is for you. I see you, understand you, and am here for you. I hope it empowers you to step boldly into your own strength, igniting the confidence within you. Remember, every life-changing journey begins with one courageous step.

To my cherished family and friends, thank you for being my anchors and guiding lights. Thank you, Chris, for our amazing children. To my wonderful children, Caden, Jordan, and Claire, you are my joy and my constant inspiration; I love you to the moon and back.

To my grandmas, Margaret Weger and MaryAnn Moeller, for their generations of wisdom and love they have shared with me. To all my aunts: Kathie Sergent, Rebecca Maurer, Carolyn Weger, Sheila Weger, Kathy Blanchard, Rhonda Markowsky, Lorelie Carey, and Gerri Moeller for being incredible role models and teaching me about life.

Thank you to my mom, Brenda Moeller, and my sister, Jenna Moeller Carvalho—your unwavering support and strength have grounded me throughout my entire life. Thank you to my dad, Larry Moeller, and brothers, Lee Moeller and Helder Carvalho, for supporting my dreams. And to my niece Audrey and nephew James Carvalho for all of your love.

To my extraordinary friends—Adelina Fabiano, Amanda Hunsley, Brooke Miller, Candice Mathewson, Carol De-Luca, Cecy Martinez, Courtney Sproule, Divina Oliverio, Jennifer Barroll, Josephine Tite, Leslie Crozier, Louisa Salomons, Maria Bellotto, Monica Ila, Nicoletta Renzi, Shaima Ibrahim, Tiffany Lucas, and Valentina Renzi—your friendship and encouragement lift me higher than words can express. I love being around strong and inspiring women who look for greatness in each other. To my sister friend Anna Sarkisovva, it has been an honor walking beside you.

A heartfelt thank you to my writing coach, AJ Harper, and Laura Stone for your invaluable guidance, support, and encouragement to help me cross the finish line. Immense gratitude to my publisher, the dedicated team at Page Two, whose expertise and excellence made this book a reality. Thank you for believing in my dreams and making them achievable goals.

Thank you to my team: Adam Conlin, Claire Masikewich, Danae Gibbons, Denise Nerier, Gina Aschenbrener, Taylor McNeill, Vika Hushchenko, and Vishal Joshi. Shout-out to Erin Skye Kelly for believing in me. Thank you Paula Onysko and Stevie Borne for your support. Thank you to my amazing photographer, Sarah Chin.

Thank you to my Mamasita, Claudia, for always encouraging me to live my dreams. To Allie and Gaby: may you always remember to be courageous like your mom.

To all of my dancers, teachers, parents, and soul sisters that I have had the privilege of working with at Soul Connexion. It has been an honor watching you shine. The skills you have learned in dance will carry you far beyond the studio walls.

Writing a book is no small feat, and I am grateful for the support of all who contributed to this collective endeavor, including my advanced readers and the wonderful women I have had the honor of coaching. To the new friends I met along this journey—you blessed me with your kindness and shared belief in my work. Amazing things happen when we follow our calling with courage.

To all the women and girls who will turn these pages: let's embrace the chance to make Big Freakin' Changes together. Change is an invitation to elevate ourselves and, through it, each other. Let's reimagine our relationship with change and allow it to lead us to the next, truest versions of ourselves.

The stories in this book are inspired by real-life experiences, thoughtfully adapted to honor the commonalities that unite us all. May they inspire you to take action, to embrace growth, and to make your BFC a reality.

NOTES

1. The Change You Want

p. 10 *less than 9 percent of small businesses break one million dollars in revenue:* Small Business Majority, "Digital Transformation: Small Businesses Face Obstacles, Opportunities in Utilizing Digital Accounting Software," November 7, 2023, smallbusinessmajority.org/sites/default/files/research-reports/toplines-small-businesses-obstacles-opportunities-digital-accounting-software.pdf.

p. 10 *less than 2 percent of all businesses are women-owned:* Eilene Zimmerman, "Only 2% of Women-Owned Businesses Break the $1 Million Mark—Here's How to Be One of Them," *Forbes*, April 1, 2015, forbes.com/sites/eilenezimmerman/2015/04/01/only-2-of-women-owned-businesses-break-the-1-million-mark-heres-how-to-be-one-of-them.

p. 10 *"at the current rate of progress, it will take 286 years:* Marianne Schnall, "Gender Equality Is Achievable in Our Lifetime: New Book Reveals How Laws Directly Impact Equality and the Global Economy," *Forbes*, March 21, 2023, forbes.com/sites/marianneschnall/2023/03/21/gender-equality-is-achievable-in-our-lifetime-new-book-reveals-how-laws-directly-impact-equality-and-the-global-economy.

p. 11 *women have 80 percent of autoimmune disease because of:* Your Inner Child Matters, "Why 80% of Autoimmune Sufferers Are Women?" YouTube, 6:35, April 21, 2023, youtube.com/watch?v=taYvjQ0_ldA.

p. 11 *the evident differences in empathy between women and men:* Leonardo Christov-Moore et al., "Empathy: Gender Effects in Brain and Behavior," *Neuroscience & Biobehavioral Reviews* 46, no. 4 (October 2014): 604–27, doi.org/10.1016/j.neubiorev.2014.09.001.

p. 13   *success correlates greater with confidence than competence:* Katty Kay and Claire Shipman, "It's Not Enough to Be Good," *The Confidence Code: The Science and Art of Self-Assurance—What Women Should Know* (HarperCollins, 2018).

p. 13   *"It isn't that women don't have the ability to succeed:* Kay and Shipman, "Introduction," *The Confidence Code.*

p. 13   *"We do a lot more ruminating than men":* Kay and Shipman, "'Dumb Ugly Bitches' and Other Reasons Women Have Less Confidence," *The Confidence Code.*

p. 14   *psychological traits might influence these differences in risk aversion and ambiguity aversion:* Lex Borghans et al., "Gender Differences in Risk Aversion and Ambiguity Aversion," *Journal of the European Economic Association* 7, nos. 2–3 (April–May 2009): 649–58, jstor.org/stable/40282781.

p. 25   *"Self-confidence is the belief in your abilities as a person:* Jamie Kern Lima, *Worthy: How to Believe You Are Enough and Transform Your Life* (Hay House, 2024), 23.

2. Courage to Change

p. 31   *over 75 percent of people feel "stuck" personally and professionally:* Caroline Castrillon, "10 Tips to Stop Feeling Stuck in Your Career," *Forbes,* January 22, 2023, forbes.com/sites/caroline castrillon/2023/01/22/10-tips-to-stop-feeling-stuck-in-your-career/.

p. 31   *"autonomy [is] critical to people's wellbeing, happiness and mental health:* Tracy Brower, "The Power of Choice and What Matters Most for the Future of Work," *Forbes,* February 21, 2021, forbes.com/sites/tracybrower/2021/02/21/the-power-of-choice-and-what-matters-most-for-the-future-of-work.

p. 31   *close to 80 percent of women struggle with low self-esteem:* Christine L. Exley and Judd B. Kessler, "The Gender Gap in Self-Promotion," *Quarterly Journal of Economics* 137, no. 3 (August 2022): 1345–81, doi.org/10.1093/qje/qjac003.

p. 35   *"Women encounter the 'mirrored door' at some point in our careers:* Ellen Connelly Taaffe, *The Mirrored Door: Break Through the Hidden Barrier That Locks Successful Women in Place* (Page Two, 2023), back cover copy, 44.

p. 40   *"If you are feeling stuck, you are not lost:* Elizabeth Gilbert in a group call with the Dance Studio Owners Association's Inner Circle Mastery program on December 1, 2023.

3. Types of Change

p. 56   *95 percent of all our decisions are "shaped by emotion":* Dylan Walsh, "Faculty: Baba Shiv, The Sanwa Bank, Limited, Professor of Marketing," Stanford Graduate School of Business, October 9, 2019, gsb.stanford.edu/faculty-research/faculty/voices/baba-shiv.

p. 61   *wellness has eight mutually interdependent aspects:* "8 Dimensions of Wellness," *Your Guide to Living Well* (blog), University of Maryland, umwellness.wordpress.com/8-dimensions-of-wellness.

p. 61   *"Attention must be given to all the dimensions:* Debbie L. Stoewen, "Dimensions of Wellness: Change Your Habits, Change Your Life," *Canadian Veterinary Journal* 58, no. 8 (August 2017): 861–62, ncbi.nlm.nih.gov/pmc/articles/PMC5508938.

4. Update Your Mindset

p. 73   *the average person has roughly sixty thousand thoughts every single day:* Christine Comaford, "Got Inner Peace? 5 Ways to Get It NOW," *Forbes*, November 7, 2013, forbes.com/sites/christinecomaford/2012/04/04/got-inner-peace-5-ways-to-get-it-now.

p. 76   *"Change your thoughts. Change your life":* Wayne W. Dyer, *Change Your Thoughts—Change Your Life: Living the Wisdom of the Tao* (Hay House, 2007).

p. 77   *Adopting a growth mindset means choosing possibilities:* Kim Armstrong, "Carol Dweck on How Growth Mindsets Can Bear Fruit in the Classroom," *Observer*, Association for Psychological Science, October 29, 2019, psychologicalscience.org/observer/dweck-growth-mindsets.

5. Small Steps, Massive Change

p. 104   *if we get just 1 percent better every day, we will become thirty-seven times better after one year:* James Clear, *Atomic Habits: An Easy & Proven Way to Build Good Habits & Break Bad Ones* (Penguin, 2018), 15.

p. 105   *how "tiny changes" create "remarkable results":* Clear, *Atomic Habits*.

p. 105   *Clear suggests these four rules to make it stick:* Clear, *Atomic Habits*, 55.

p. 113   *"Your future growth and progress are now based in your understanding:* Dan Sullivan quoted in Benjamin Hardy, "This Is the Secret to Finding Happiness and Confidence while Pursuing Goals," *Inc.*, May 21, 2018, inc.com/benjamin-p-hardy/this-is-secret-to-finding-happiness-confidence-while-pursuing-goals.html.

6. Rest, Reflect, Protect

p. 123 *"Stringently adhering to cultural norms at the expense of your own passions:* Adrian R. Camilleri, "The 6 Most Common Regrets People Experience," *Psychology Today*, June 11, 2021, psychologytoday.com/intl/blog/life-s-biggest-decisions/202106/the-6-most-common-regrets-people-experience.

p. 124 *"The 'resting' brain turns out to be consolidating memories:* Alex Soojung-Kim Pang, *Rest: Why You Get More Done When You Work Less* (Basic Books, 2016), 32.

p. 126 *"The brain automatically switches on a default mode network:* Pang, *Rest*, 35.

p. 130 *Studies also show that gratitude:* Madhuleena Roy Chowdhury, "The Neuroscience of Gratitude and Effects on the Brain," PositivePsychology.com, last updated September 19, 2024, positivepsychology.com/neuroscience-of-gratitude/#brain-effects.

p. 137 *Neuroscientist Antonio Damasio has called humans "feeling machines that think":* Justin James Kennedy, "Is Emotional Curiosity the Key?" *Psychology Today*, November 11, 2020, psychologytoday.com/ca/blog/brain-reboot/202011/is-emotional-curiosity-the-key.

p. 137 *"Healthy boundaries are generous and efficient:* Terri Cole, "Your Turn," *Boundary Boss: The Essential Guide to Talk True, Be Seen, and (Finally) Live Free* (Sounds True, 2021).

p. 138 *"Personal boundaries are like a guidebook that you create:* Cole, "Personal Boundaries 101," *Boundary Boss*.

7. Act Boldly

p. 150 *"Past behaviour or habit, and psychological reactance:* Niamh Murtagh, Birgitta Gatersleben, and David Uzzell, "Self-Identity Threat and Resistance to Change: Evidence from Regular Travel Behaviour," *Journal of Environmental Psychology* 32, no. 4 (December 2012): 318–26, doi.org/10.1016/j.jenvp.2012.05.008.

p. 150 *we are the average of the five people we spend the most time with:* Aimee Groth, "You're the Average of the Five People You Spend the Most Time With," *Business Insider*, July 24, 2012, businessinsider.com/jim-rohn-youre-the-average-of-the-five-people-you-spend-the-most-time-with-2012-7.

p. 152 *In* Verywell Mind, *the four main archetypes he identified are:* Kendra Cherry, "What Are the Jungian Archetypes?" *Verywell Mind*, last updated May 5, 2024, verywellmind.com/what-are-jungs-4-major-archetypes-2795439.

p. 152   *"notion of the independent, coherent self is an illusion:* Descriptive copy for Bruce Hood, *The Self Illusion: How the Social Brain Creates Identity* (HarperCollins, 2012), at global.oup.com/academic/product/the-self-illusion-9780199988785?cc=ca&lang=en&#.

p. 153   *"Research shows that we're more stressed when:* Maya Shankar, "Why Change Is So Scary—and How to Unlock Its Potential," TED Talk, 13:31, April 2023, ted.com/talks/maya_shankar_why_change_is_so_scary_and_how_to_unlock_its_potential.

p. 153   *Shankar encourages us to focus on the expansiveness of change and provides three questions:* Shankar, "Why Change Is So Scary."

p. 154   *"Any action is often better than no action:* Eckhart Tolle, *The Power of Now: A Guide to Spiritual Enlightenment* (New World Library, 1999), 69.

p. 155   *"Between stimulus and response lies a space:* "Alleged Quote," Viktor Frankl Institut, viktorfrankl.org/quote_stimulus.html.

p. 155   *"When we are no longer able to change a situation:* Viktor Frankl, *Man's Search for Meaning* (Touchstone, 1984), 116.

p. 157   *it takes us ninety seconds to identify an emotion and allow it to dissipate:* Bryan E. Robinson, "The 90-Second Rule That Builds Self-Control," *Psychology Today*, April 26, 2020, psychologytoday.com/ca/blog/the-right-mindset/202004/the-90-second-rule-builds-self-control.

8. Joy in the Journey

p. 167   *"We are human beings, not human doings":* Rick Warren, *The Purpose Driven Life: What on Earth Am I Here For?*, expanded ed. (Zondervan, 2012), 177.

p. 171   *"Authenticity is the daily practice of letting go of:* Brené Brown, *The Gifts of Imperfection: Let Go of Who You Think You're Supposed to Be and Embrace Who You Are* (Hazelden, 2010), 50.

9. Unlock Your Confidence

p. 187   *In her Emotion Wheel II, she identifies eleven core human emotions:* See Dr. S. Colby Peters's Emotion Wheel II in "Build Mindfulness Skills with Our Emotion Wheels and Needs Wheels," Human Systems, humansystems.co/emotionwheels/.

p. 188   *"feeling the fear and doing it anyway":* Oprah Winfrey, "Courage is…" Facebook post, April 2, 2012, facebook.com/oprahwinfrey/posts/courage-is-feeling-the-fear-and-doing-it-anyway/221105204663913.

p. 188   *"confidence is embodied in action":* Mel Robbins, "A Toolkit for Confidence: How to Build UNSHAKABLE Self Confidence,"

The Mel Robbins Podcast, YouTube, 55:13, March 6, 2023, youtube.com/watch?v=kMtNkJcJn3M.

p. 189 *"You're not crazy, you're just first":* Jamie Kern Lima, "You're Not Crazy, You're Just First!" YouTube, 9:11, December 5, 2023, youtube.com/watch?v=f6rhAlMJXGI.

p. 189 *"Michelle Obama is the bravest of women:* Aimee Stern, "Michelle Obama Is Not Always Brave," Thrive Global, December 30, 2018, community.thriveglobal.com/michelle-obamas-becoming-is-so-brave.

p. 189 *"I never felt beautiful:* Jenny Bailly, "Lady Gaga: The Power of Makeup," *Allure*, September 12, 2019, allure.com/story/lady-gaga-cover-story-power-of-makeup.

p. 190 *"having the knowledge, confidence, means, or ability:* "Empowered," *Merriam-Webster Dictionary*, merriam-webster.com/dictionary/empowered.

p. 190 *created Wonder Woman as the first female superhero:* Christopher Klein, "Wonder Woman's Surprising WWII-Era Origins," History, last updated May 16, 2023, history.com/news/wonder-woman-origins.

10. Stepping Into Greatness

p. 221 *"Life isn't about waiting for the storm to pass:* "Interview with Vivian Greene on Learning to Dance in the Rain and More," ChiTAG Group, chitag.com/single-post/2017/02/13/interview-with-vivian-greene.

SARAH CHIN PHOTOGRAPHY

ABOUT THE AUTHOR

CARA MOELLER POPPITT is an accomplished leader dedicated to helping people break through barriers, take bold actions, and achieve their highest aspirations. With twenty-five years of experience as a dancer and choreographer, she understands the powerful connection between mindset, movement, and transformation—both in individuals and organizations.

As the founder of two award-winning companies, Cara ranks among the top 2 percent of female entrepreneurs, a testament to her visionary leadership and strategic insight. She has guided over ten thousand entrepreneurs toward unlocking their full potential, combining creativity with business acumen to drive growth and innovation.

Cara's accolades include being named Global TV's Woman of Vision and CIBC's Entrepreneur of the Year, along with features on Global News. Based in Calgary, Alberta, Canada, she continues to inspire people worldwide, delivering results-oriented coaching and speaking that drives meaningful change.

THE JOURNEY DOESN'T END HERE

THANK YOU for reading *Big Freakin' Change*! I'd love to stay connected and continue celebrating your wins, big and small. Follow me on Instagram at **@caramoellerpoppitt**, where we can share those moments of action and transformation together.

Ready for More?

- Download the *Big Freakin' Change* workbook, designed to help you put the concepts into practice. You can grab it directly from **bigfreakinchange.com**!

- Tune in to my *Big Freakin' Change* podcast.

- Listen to the audiobook: If you're someone who absorbs messages best by listening, the *Big Freakin' Change* audiobook is waiting for you—available wherever audiobooks are sold. Let it be your on-the-go inspiration!

Spread the Word!

If *Big Freakin' Change* resonated with you, I'd be incredibly grateful for a review. You can share your feedback on your favorite online retailer's website. Don't forget to use the hashtag #bigfreakinchange on social media so I can see how you're embracing change!

If you think another woman could benefit from the message in this book, consider getting her a copy. Remember, when people around us rise, we all rise.

Bring Me In—Let's Work Together

I've got all the tools you need to keep moving forward. Here are a few ways I can help:

- Group and private coaching.
- Corporate training.
- Speaking: My keynote covers the Get Unstuck, Cycle of Change Model in a digestible, action-packed format perfect for any audience.

Just scan the QR code below or head to bigfreakinchange.com to explore all the ways I can support your journey.

www.ingramcontent.com/pod-product-compliance
Lightning Source LLC
LaVergne TN
LVHW030241250326
834688LV00047B/1755